The Financial Freedom Formula

The Financial Freedom Formula

*How to become financially free
and live the life you want*

MARTIN DODD

THE CHOIR PRESS

First published in the United Kingdom in 2019 by
The Choir Press

ISBN 978-1-78963-053-4

To my dad for getting me started on this journey, and my mum for always believing in me.

To Sally, for unswerving encouragement.

To Harriet and James for challenging me to see things differently.

Contents

Contents

1　Introduction

The secret of getting ahead is getting started
– Mark Twain

Let's get straight into the serious and exciting business of creating FINAN-CIAL FREEDOM for you and your family. Probably one of the most important journeys we all need to make as everything we do in life is affected by how much financial security we have. Clearly having enough money is not the answer to every problem, however money is very useful in helping solve problems and providing us with great peace of mind that no matter what happens in our lives, we have the resources to deal with it. That would not only be very satisfying, but also very liberating, wouldn't you agree?

As you can probably tell, this is not an enormous book by any means, it's not a 500-page epic. This is a short book with loads of ideas and immediate calls to action that you can start using today to start your journey to financial freedom, or get even better if you are already on the way. It is full of very important strategies that anyone can apply today immediately, no theories or technical jargon that will leave you feeling confused and disillusioned. Everything in this book is real and not a theory.

I have personally read more business, mentoring, mindset and financial coaching books than I care to remember, but the problem with most of them is this: They are just far too long, take far too long to get to the point – and that is assuming that you even get to finish reading the book.

When I first started writing this book, my intention was to get right to the point and very quickly. My belief is that too many of us don't know where to start or what to do when it comes to planning for a much better financial future. When we don't understand something clearly or well enough it usually means we try to avoid it, or at least avoid it as long as possible. And delaying is most definitely our enemy. The more time we have to work on our financial goals, the better the chance of a successful outcome.

Many of us have not been taught what we need to know about financial freedom. We haven't had the right education at school, that in any way helps us prepare for a better future. That is in no way a criticism of our education system; the topic is just not given, in my opinion, enough priority at the moment. I do believe, however, that if better financial education was a priority in schools, we would see much better-informed choices being made.

I will get right to the point, keep you engaged and hopefully inspire you to start, or re-start if you have stalled, to continue your journey to financial freedom. I want you to take personal responsibility for your financial future. We will all be more satisfied, more content with our lives once we start on this journey, and the trick is to not only start, but to keep going. Part of keeping going is knowing and understanding the rules, and to keep applying them. Now, some of you may not have realised that there is a set of rules, and I am here to tell you that there are, and most of the people who have achieved financial freedom either know these rules or have, by a quirk of fate, followed these rules.

Let's get this out there first and foremost: There is no knight in shining armour that is going to come riding to our rescue, so we all need to face the truth. For most of us, we have to create our own financial freedom and financial security. For those of us who have already mastered some degree of financial security and have already achieved it, there is always opportunity to up your game, to improve your game and to get to the next level. My belief is that the more financially secure we are, the more able we are to not only help our family and friends, but we are also great advocates to those around us who can benefit from our knowledge and wisdom. Everyone I know would be excited to take advice from a successful person. Surely, we all want to know their secret. The truth is, there is no one secret, but there are rules that we can all follow that can help us on our journey and help us avoid making too many mistakes. Yes, we will make mistakes on the way, but more about that later.

So, let's get started.

2 Taking responsibility

The trouble is, you think you have time

– Buddha

Why is financial freedom important? In fact, why should any of us regard it as anything that we should worry about all? In one word, we can sum it up as 'responsibility'. Responsibility to ourselves, to our families and to our communities.

Have you ever thought, 'I want to be financially free and not to have to worry about money'?

Of course, you have. In fact, we all have, or at the very least wished we had more money behind us. There is something deeply comforting about having a bit behind you that helps you sleep a little better at night.

I am pretty sure that at some point in your life you have worried about money, and maybe it's a thought that you have regularly, especially if you are reading this book. Some of the thoughts that go through our heads are, 'I am worried that I may not have enough money to pay the rent or the mortgage this month', or maybe you are worried that you may have to work long past a normal retirement age because you just can't afford to retire. There are many other financial questions that cause us concern and sleepless nights, and if we could just find the answer, we would feel so much better about ourselves.

But imagine how you would feel if you could achieve financial freedom sooner rather than later. And imagine how you would feel if you were confident that you had not only a great strategy in place, but also a plan to follow that was going to ensure that you achieved your goal of financial freedom.

I am certain that you would be a more confident person and you would be a happier person for taking the responsibility to reach out for your goals. Not only that, but people around you would want to know what you know. Just about everyone I know has at the very least a sneaking admiration for someone who is successful. It of course goes without saying that I am talking about people who have become financially successful through good old honest hard work, achieved through entirely legal and moral ways. We should not be interested or concerned with people whose wealth has been achieved through ill-gotten gains. In any case, the universe usually has a way of catching up with these people in the end.

Why should you start working on your own personal financial freedom today? Why do we need to start dealing with it right now? After all, there are far more interesting things to do today, instead of working on this 'thing' we call financial freedom. Well, I can tell you that there are two parts to answering that question. Firstly, for most of us this will take some time and certainly some persistence. Of course, we all know of people that have achieved amazing success in a very short period of time, but they are really very rare and unusual. The norm is that financial freedom takes time to plan and certainly time to execute. So, we have to be patient and let time do some of the work for us.

And secondly, those people who are an overnight success – many of them succumb to financial problems in the future. Quick success when it comes to money matters can trick us into believing that it is easy and that we have the "Midas" touch. Putting it very simply, what comes easy is often not appreciated until it's gone. This is especially true of young people that achieve success and then find that when things get difficult, it is often harder for them to pick up the pieces and start again.

Being patient on our journey to financial freedom is one discipline we need and to not waver from. Many people are just too impatient for results and are easily derailed and give up far too soon, blaming the system, or other people around them, for causing them to lose their way or give up alto-gether. Being patient is definitely our friend when it comes to financial freedom.

Thinking about it and achieving it are two very different things and I think that we would all agree that getting to that point of financial freedom is often challenging and a long and sometimes lonely road. For sure it's a path that is not well trodden.

But imagine what life would be like when you get there – more time to do the things you enjoy doing, more time with your family, more holidays, more time to spend on your hobbies … I could go on.

If this sounds like where you want to get to, read on. This book is for you.

3 Getting from 'A' to 'B'

Failing to plan is planning to fail

— Benjamin Franklin

Have you ever had one of those moments or days in your life that changed the way you think about things? Some of us have and some of us haven't, but if you have, you will know they can have a life-long effect on us. Sometimes an event can have a deep effect on us, but it is not until years later that we realise how much of an impact it had.

Here's a story about getting things wrong – really wrong.

If you were with me on 26th April 1996, you'd have seen me broken and in a lot of pain. My legs had been cramping for what seemed like hours. Lying on the cold, damp golden gravel of Horse Guards Parade, I was feeling utterly miserable, and 'disappointed in myself' was nothing short of an understatement. We have all had times in our lives when we have felt like that.

In that moment, I became aware that someone was standing over me, and I had already guessed what was coming next.

'Where have you been for so long? Did you stop off on the way?' The questions were almost being fired at me.

Looking up slowly, I turned to the person looming over me …

'You've no idea how tough a run that was. You've never done it. You should try it for yourself,' I said, feeling very defensive and miserable at the same time.

The person grilling me, a lean-built authoritative man, was my father. A man who rarely raised his voice to anyone, a man who was of medium height, commanded instant respect, even though he was in his late fifties. A man of strong self-discipline, carved out of a tough post-war upbringing and a stint in the British Army doing national service.

You see, I am lying on the golden gravel of Horse Guards Parade at the back of Whitehall, London in a great deal of pain after battling through a five-hour London Marathon. Even to this day, I wonder how I managed to get to the finish line. I thought I was fit enough to more than comfortably complete a marathon, having exercised daily all my life.

So, how did I end up there in the first place? Let me take you back to the year before.

A year earlier I was at the funeral of a close family friend who tragically died at the age of thirty-two from Hodgkin lymphoma. It is often in times like this that we have crazy – and sometimes great – ideas. Out of nowhere, the famous last words where uttered from my brother's mouth.

'Why don't we run London Marathon next year and raise money for the Lymphoma Society? It's the least we can do.'

'Great idea, we should definitely do that,' I said.

To put this into perspective, my brother was not particularly into exercise, let alone a marathon runner.

Our applications were submitted and months later we miraculously both received confirmation that we had both been accepted into the race the following year.

'Wow, how did that happen? If you get a place in the marathon, you are one of the lucky few,' people said. Even back in 1995.

As I was exercising every day, I thought the race was not going to be a major challenge. How could running a marathon be all that difficult? Or so I thought. Hey, it was all going to be easy and I would be helping a great cause.

Training commenced in the New Year of 1996. A few runs a week, and a long run was completed on Fridays.

Of course, a few people did suggest that I take this project a lot more seriously. More than a few people suggested that I really should follow a properly structured training program, get the right shoes, and eat the right sort of food. As you can imagine, a lot of this fell on deaf ears.

'What do I need to do all that for? I exercise every day and have done for years and years. I don't need any help and I will be able to do it no problem. In fact, I am going for a fast time,' I said.

I never quite worked out how far my training runs were, just kept a check of how long I was out running and convinced myself that I was running well. It turned out months down the line that my longest run before marathon day was a paltry 11 miles!

So, marathon day arrived – 20th April. It started out as a perfect day for marathon running: a cool damp, drizzly, grey day.

'So, Mark, how are you going to go today?'

'It's going to be really tough. I've done nowhere near enough training.'

I, on the other hand, was full of self-confidence and that little internal voice we all have was feeling rather confident. 'Martin,' I thought to myself, 'you are going to fly around and be sitting drinking beer well before Mark gets back.'

The only other people at the start, at Blackfriars, were runners and they all looked like they'd turned up in their underpants! Proper kit! Hmmm, maybe I should have listened to the advice after all. Around me everyone was limbering up and stretching. Eventually as the clock moved towards the 9.30 start time, I wished my brother good luck as the marshals shepherded us to the start. It looked like chaos to me, but who was I to judge?

At 9.30 the cannon fired, and 30,000 runners were off on the journey through the streets of London. Bounding along, running tall, gazelle like. This was going to be a great day – or so I thought.

Maybe I was naive, but I very soon realised that this was going to be one very long day. At just three miles my legs started to ache – yes, just three miles – and I felt like I had not prepared properly or done anything like the right amount of training.

The internal voice started in my head: 'Maybe it will pass … Maybe I'm injured … but it doesn't feel like that.' All sorts of questions started to come into my head. Yes, this was going to be a long, long day.

There were no supporters at the side of the road to encourage the runners yet, thankfully! But it was really lonely and all the runners around me were in their own worlds. By the time I reached London Bridge, my pace had slowed to almost a crawl and was running more like a lumbering chimpanzee than a gazelle. And to dent my pride even further, I was passed by a charity running gorilla! Yes, I was with the charity runners, not that there is anything wrong with that. Let me tell you, being passed by a runner wearing a hairy jumpsuit and mask is no fun. Crossing London Bridge, I could see the runners further along the course passing under the road just before the bridge, a whole eight miles ahead of me! How could I be so far behind?

'Depressing or what!'

I was getting slower and slower by the mile and my legs began to take on the feeling of being gripped in a vice. I was in ever more pain as I struggled from mile to mile and feed station to feed station, in the vain hope that some energy drink would miraculously take the pain away from my legs. I can tell you: it didn't. Soldiering on, from the halfway point I walked, staggered and shuffled, doing anything other than run, and yet there were few people to encourage the runners on as I edged closer to the finish.

'These legs just do not belong to me anymore!'

At last I reached the Embankment approaching Westminster Bridge, where I was passed by more runners, charity runners and yet more people in fancy dress costumes!

'What a disaster.'

Saying I'd failed to plan and prepare properly would have been the under-statement of the year.

And I started to wonder what my family waiting at the finish line would be thinking – 'Had my brother passed me? Would any of them still be there? And how am I going to get through this to the finish?' A head full of questions.

Turning right at Westminster Bridge, I could see Big Ben and knew that I was going to get to the finish, even if I had to crawl.

For the first time on the route there were now crowds of people, and as I turned onto Birdcage Walk the crowds were cheering at me – why, I have no idea. This was no victory for me of any kind. The problem, though, was that I was barely moving forward. Even though hours had passed, the crowds were kindly offering every encouragement. If the ground had opened up, I would have jumped in the hole.

11

'Keep going! You can do it!'

'Only a mile to go! You're nearly there!'

Except, it wasn't a great achievement. As far as I was concerned, it was a massive disappointment.

Turning into the Mall, I could see the finish line as I staggered along. A finish, yes, but not the one I had hoped for.

I could have cried, if it wasn't for my legs hurting so much. Not only that, my pride was severely dented too.

Eventually I found my mum and my dad as I stumbled and staggered around Horse Guards Parade, then collapsed in a heap. Despite my father's interrogation, my parents, for some reason, were extremely proud of my achievement and that, at least, made me feel like I had achieved something. Within a few minutes Mark appeared looking equally as shattered as I felt. It had been a tough day for him as well.

So, what do think happened next?

Well, there was the inevitable inquest.

Many a comment like, 'I told you so, but you wouldn't listen to me. I knew this was going to happen.' And you can probably guess the rest. It was a huge lesson for me.

Surprisingly, after performing well below how I had hoped, the very next week I entered another marathon. What kind of a fool does that? This one, obviously. With the right planning and preparation, the next time was going to be different, very different. I'd well and truly learnt my lesson.

So, to cut a long story short, I started to follow a proper coaching program, bought the right kit and even started to eat a proper diet. My follow-up marathon and subsequent running events and triathlons went very differently, and to this day I still regularly compete in endurance events.

So, you may be wondering: What does marathon running have to do with financial planning?

Well, for me it taught me a very important lesson, not only in terms of running but also how I looked at planning and preparing for anything I did. If I was to successfully achieve any of my own personal goals and ambitions, proper planning was going to be essential in order for success to follow. I didn't matter if it was in sport or in pursuit of financial freedom, I had to have a plan!

We often start out in life not really knowing what we want to achieve or where we want to get to. And it's very easy to just let life take its course. Many of us accidentally fall into the trap of not really planning and just living from one year to the next.

It is easy to fall into the mindset of 'I don't need to do it just yet. I'm far too young for that. I'll do it in a few years' time.'

Sometimes the planning bit never happens and suddenly you are two-thirds of the way through your life and wondering where all the time has gone. Have you ever wondered were all the years went?

Imagine what life could be like, though, if you had a plan. A plan that was targeted towards your dreams and goals. Goals that are your personal aspirations and your objectives. Maybe having a plan would make all the difference.

4 Not a sprint, this is a marathon

It takes twenty years to make an overnight success
— Eddie Cantor

In an age of instant news, social media and a 'must have it all' attitude, we can be forgiven for being impatient for success, whether that is in our careers, the success of our favourite sports team and especially how much money we have in the bank. We all know the stories of famous entrepreneurs, none more so than people like Steve Jobs, Bill Gates and Mark Zuckerberg, launching massively successful companies and becoming fabulously wealthy beyond just about everyone's wildest dreams. Mark Zuckerberg started Facebook from his Harvard dormitory before he even reached his twentieth birthday. Today, he is one of the richest people in the world. It is hardly surprising that most of us are hungry for success, and we want it now.

The problem, though, is this: There are very few Mark Zuckerbergs, Steve Jobs or Bill Gates in this world and only a handful come along every generation. And because their success is clearly visible for everyone to see, we are in danger of becoming impatient for success ourselves. We want to be successful now, wanting all the trappings of a successful life right now, but for the vast majority of us, that is not going to happen.

Sadly, there are people out there who know that there are lots of very hungry people looking for that 'golden arrow' that is going to bring them financial freedom and success and unfortunately will prey on people selling them the latest get-rich-quick schemes that are going to transform their lives, quite literally overnight, with very little effort. BUT funnily enough they all come with an upfront fee which is usually very expensive! Unfortunately, if something looks too good to be true, it probably is. In fact, in my own experience, I would go as far as saying that if it looks too good to be true then it isn't likely to help you to become successful at all. Tempting as these schemes may be, my advice is to steer clear of them at all cost. Talking of which, to acquire the knowledge from these get-rich-quick schemes, whilst costing a lot of money, almost always ends in failure, and it is virtually impossible to get your money back.

So, what's the answer?

The answer is, in many ways, a very simple one. And there are only two simple steps.

First you must start and then you must keep going!

The problem, however, is that many of us put off starting for far too long in the first place. How many times have we not fully started because we don't think we need to start just yet, only to see years pass us by and only finally decide we must do something when we can almost see the finish line looming on the horizon?

And secondly, once we do start it is sometimes easy to lose faith in the journey when it has only just begun and give up. Let me give you an example. A young man decides that he should be saving for his future and puts £50 away in a savings account. At the end of the year his savings have not grown that much and are worth only £630 with interest and growth. Looking at the sum of money, he thinks how much more fun he would have had spending the £50 each month and after all, if he is only going to save £600 a year, he asks himself 'what's the point?' and gives up before he's really begun. So, he gives up and enjoys the money now instead. We can all probably tell that his chances of ever achieving financial freedom are very small. Don't let that be you.

Impatient for success, the young man was thinking of his money as a sprint race, but imagine if he thought of his money as a marathon. Imagine if he thought, 'I need to keep going and doing as much as I can, for as long as I can'? And imagine if he was an ambitious young man and his career progressed, earning a promotion and a higher salary after a few years. He then saved much more than £50 a month, and so over time the amount invested, doubled, trebled and quadrupled. I don't need to do the maths, as you can see over time his investment portfolio would grow and grow.

Unfortunately, too many of us are sprinting towards financial freedom, which rarely works, rather than looking at financial freedom as a marathon to be embraced. As Jim Rohn said, 'Successful people do what unsuccessful people are not willing to do. Don't wish it were easier; wish you were better.'

In my words, to be successful and achieve financial freedom, you have to do what you've got to do, as there are no shortcuts to success. You must stay on the path to success and not stop by the roadside.

5 You must have a plan

A goal in your head is just a dream. A dream written down is a plan of action

– Martin Dodd

We are all dreamers. We all have aspirations about the things we'd like to do, the places we'd like to visit and the things we'd like to have. None of us should be ashamed to admit that; it's a human characteristic common to us all, even though every one of us has a unique set of dreams. There is nothing wrong with having dreams, the dreams we have in our heads that we only ever talk to ourselves about. Sometimes, in fact most of the time, the dreams we have we do not even share with our partners in life and there is a very good reason why we don't share them. And even if we do, we often talk about them in a half-hearted way, reserving our really big dreams for those self-talk conversations. You know the ones I mean.

So, why do we not share our dreams and aspirations?

It's really quite simple. Big goals are scary enough even when we talk about them to ourselves, but sharing them with other people lays us open to criticism, ridicule, negative talk and jealousy. So, it's hardly surprising that our innermost dreams are more often than not, kept locked away in our heads. And therein lies the problem. A dream is just that: a dream. A dream that may never take seed, may never be acted upon and may never ever begin to happen. Interestingly, most of the world's billionaires are self-made. I would wager that these people were big dreamers and wrote down their plans/dreams.

If we accept that our innermost dreams and ambitions are hard to share even with our family and loved ones, we need to find a way to turn our dreams into an action plan for the future.

How can we do this?

The best way to formulate your dreams into an action plan is to write down your goals, and that can be a paper version, on your laptop or on your phone. To help start your list of goals there are a few simple steps to take. Think about your goals over different timescales. Firstly, think about your short-term goals, the goals that you wish to achieve in the next twelve months. Secondly, think about your medium-term goals, goals that you wish to achieve in the next five years. And finally, think about your long-term goals, goals that you wish to achieve fifteen to twenty years from now.

There is a really important reason to break down your goals over time which is that it's natural to think about our long-term goals at the expense of our short- and medium-term goals. These goals are just as important in the journey to financial freedom because they help keep us on track to the long-term goals and they help keep us enthusiastic and engaged with the bigger picture. Short- and medium-term goals are the marking posts on our journey to success and are rewards to ourselves. They help remind us what we are ultimately planning to achieve.

Here's an example of what an action plan might look like.

Short-term goals

1. Increase business production/turnover by 10% next year

2. Change job to a better paid position within six months

3. Repay credit card debt in full over next nine months

Medium-term goals

1. Move to larger house within three years

2. Pay off extra 30% of mortgage within three years

3. Have children's university fees fund in place within five years

Long-term goals

1. Mortgage fully repaid within fifteen years

2. Have no personal debt within fifteen years

3. Have enough money saved so I can choose to retire within twenty years

The list is a very simple example and I would encourage you to create a list of at least fifty goals that you would like to achieve during the next twenty years or so. If you have never done this before it won't be easy, but persevere as I can assure you that it is worthwhile in the end. And don't be frightened to dream big, really big. After all, this is just for you. At least for now, anyway.

Write as many goals down as possible. You will ultimately find it quite liberating. Take your time and allow your mind to run freely, as you can always edit it later. Some of the goals that you have now may ultimately fall by the wayside as they are replaced with new ones and better ones that you have not thought about just yet.

The great thing about writing down your dreams and revisiting them is that our minds subconsciously start to think and develop ideas on how we can achieve those dreams. It is the perfect antidote to those famous last words we say to ourselves, 'One day, I'd like to (you can fill in the gap)', because I know I have been guilty of talking to myself just like that in the past.

So, go ahead and spend an hour or two writing down what you have planned for your future. Go to Appendix 1 to help you get started.

6 How to increase your wealth

It is never too late to set yourself another goal or create a new vision for your future

— Damien Thomas

Broadly speaking, by the time most people reach the conventional retirement age somewhere in their mid-sixties, around 80% of them are are flat dead broke and reliant on state support and other charitable hand-outs. At the very least, most people are forced to seriously modify their lifestyle in retirement. By anyone's standards, this is rather depressing. So, if you could change this outcome surely you would.

Approximately another 15% of the population achieve some level of financial freedom by the time they retire, with some savings and investments. However, the freedom which they achieve does not last throughout their retirement years and eventually their savings diminish completely or reduce to a very modest amount, leading to them having to change their lifestyles to accommodate the reduction in their financial security.

Finally, approximately 5% of the population achieve life-long and generational financial security. That tiny percentage is a truly frightening statistic and I sincerely don't want you to be in the 95% camp. However, the figures hide a much more disturbing fact: A person's intelligence has little to do with the outcome. Studies have shown that a person's level of intelligence is not the most important factor in determining whether a person achieves financial freedom or not. In fact, studies have shown that a group of people of the same level of intelligence have just as much chance of succeeding or failing to achieve financial freedom as any other group. The reasons for this could be the subject of another book entirely; however, what we can be certain of is that how bright you are will not be the overriding factor in whether you achieve financial freedom or not.

If so many people are not achieving financial freedom, we should perhaps first understand the ways to increase our wealth. Before jumping in, I can tell you that there are only eight ways to do this.

Yes, there are only eight ways to increase your wealth!

Here are a few scenarios to help illustrate the ways to get wealthy.

In no way am I being sexist in this section, because men *and* women have tried all these strategies since the beginning of time.

> **1. Marry it!** Louise is single and in her mid-thirties, having joined a successful company five years ago and earning a good income for a person of her age. However, Louise lives life to the full and is spending all her money on holidays and enjoying life. Louise lives in a rented property and intends to buy a property in the next five years but has no deposit and also has a few thousand pounds on credit cards. From the outside, it looks like Louise has it all sorted, living the good life, but Louise is very much not on the road to financial freedom.

So, what are Louise's plans to achieve her financial goals? Louise hopes to marry into wealth, as she does not want to give up her current lifestyle. This is her chosen way of achieving financial freedom.

It's not one that I would rely on, or recommend anyone else to rely on either. Furthermore, all her eggs are in one basket. This is like playing roulette: your number will either come up or it won't. And we all know what happens to most people who play roulette. Yes, they have a habit of losing, and losing big.

2. Steal it! Robert has already reached the halfway mark on his life journey and is in his early forties, having had numerous jobs over the years, most of which were middle management and paid a reasonable wage. As Robert has moved from job to job, he has little idea of what pension savings he has and did not join some of the company pension schemes that were offered to him. With little savings behind him, he is increasingly worried about his future, so desperate times lead to desperate measures. As he approaches 50, Robert hatches a plan.

So, what are Robert's plans to achieve his financial goals? Robert's plan is to steal the money from his current employer. He has identified a security loophole in his employer's accounting system that he is sure no one will notice. Good idea? Absolutely not, and not one I would recommend at all.

Unfortunately, this is more common than people realise and the offenders are nearly always caught, and the consequences are usually severe and have life-long effects.

3. Inherit it! Harry is 'the man about town'. He's a lovely chap who drives the right car, dresses well and is always seen in the right places. His parents ran an engineering business which they sold fifteen years ago and are now living off the sale proceeds. Harry doesn't know much about his mum and dad's financial affairs and even less about what they are worth, but he is sure that it's a tidy sum of money. As such, Harry doesn't work all that hard but certainly plays hard, as he's sure he will inherit more than enough when his parents are no longer here.

So, what are Harry's plans to achieve his financial goals? Harry's plan is to wait for the inheritance to come from his mum and dad. What he hasn't considered is firstly he has no idea of what his parents are worth, and secondly there is the very real chance that one if not both of his parents will end up in a care home, which they will have to pay for.

Furthermore, he doesn't realise that his mum and dad's plan is to have a great retirement and a really good go at spending the lot. They've even released equity from their home, so that is not worth much to Harry either.

All this spells disaster for Harry, and the sad thing is he will probably not know until it is far too late.

> **4. Win it!** Sonia worked hard five days a week but sadly did not earn a huge wage. Her partner had a similar job and did not earn a great deal either. Neither of them could see how they were going to achieve their dreams of financial security for themselves or their children. Like most of us, Sonia dreamt of not having to work so hard, having several holidays a year and being able to give money to her children, so that they could buy their first home.

So, what are Sonia's plans to achieve her financial goals? Sonia's plan is to play the lottery twice a week and to buy more tickets when there is a big rollover. Whilst someone somewhere eventually wins the lottery, Sonia is taking a huge gamble on winning. The number of players is so high that the chances of ever winning are very slim.

I am not a fan of playing the lottery at all as it takes away the drive we all need to improve our financial position, instead putting it all in the lap of the gods. The outcome is completely out of our control. Leave the lottery play to others; for most of us, it is only ever going to be a losing strategy.

You may well think the first four strategies are risky to say the least, and they certainly are. However, right now there are millions of people whose only financial freedom strategy is at least one of those or sometimes a few of them combined.

So, let's make sure that you are not one of those and look at the genuine ways to increase your wealth.

1. Run a business – Whether you help your employer run a business or run a business for yourself, this is probably the main source of increasing personal wealth. It helps you create wealth that not only helps you live your life today, but also creates a platform from which you can develop other strategies to increase your personal wealth and ultimately your financial freedom.

We all have to start to generate money, income and wealth to start the journey towards financial freedom. Whether you have you own business, plan to start your own business or work for someone else, this must be your foundation point. Whatever you do, do it to the very best of your ability. Most of the time in life, rewards come from hard work and effort. Maybe there's the odd exception, but what you can be sure of is that making little or no effort will definitely not improve your chances of succeeding.

2. Invest in property – Investing in property has long been a favourite of investors and should never be overlooked. The advantage of property is that it can provide us with a semi-passive income which can be effective both during our working lives and long into retirement. There are different property strategies that can broadly be placed in two categories: residential property and commercial property. Both residential and commercial property investments have their advantages and disadvantages, so seeking professional advice is essential to ensure the best possibility of success. Like any other investment strategy, there are good times and not so good times, so investing for the long term is important. Property has proved to be a very successful investment strategy for decades, but it is important to remember that property inflation – certainly in the residential sector – has far outstripped wage inflation. As such we may not see the same level of increases in value over the next few decades that we have seen in the past. So, if property is going to form part of your plans, it is important to remember that it is not a sprint, it's a marathon. Be prepared to be in it for the long haul.

3. Invest in stocks & shares – Investing in the stock market or another business is almost as old as time and for many investors can be almost a passive investment strategy, not requiring any day-to-day involvement.

Not only can stocks and shares be virtually passive but, if necessary, investors can choose to receive income payments periodically through the payment of dividends. Stock market investing is also another long-term investment strategy that is an ideal starting place for younger investors, and relatively modest amounts can be invested on regular basis and it does not require a large capital outlay to get started. Mighty oaks from little acorns grow.

The advantage of monthly investing is also that investors benefit from what is called 'pound cost averaging', but more on that later.

Unfortunately, stock market investing is often overlooked by many as it is perceived as being risky. The mainstream media have a habit of focusing on the days when the stock markets fall out of bed and rarely focus on the good times, which are just not newsworthy enough, I guess. It is certainly not to be overlooked though, despite the perceived volatility.

4. Intellectual property – We are all potential experts in our field and the longer you have worked in a particular sector, the greater the chances are that you have a knowledge base that other people will pay you good money for. Most of us don't realise this, but we could actually be sitting on a goldmine of knowledge that other people wished they had.

What's even more interesting is that the internet is now the most perfect medium to sell our intellectual knowledge to the rest of the world. There are literally no boundaries anymore.

With your unique knowledge, you can write books, create downloads, develop courses that can be sold at little cost to you, other than the time you spend putting what you have in your head into a medium for others to consume. The world is your oyster, as the saying goes.

Okay, so we have looked at the eight different ways to increase your wealth. Hopefully you are not planning on banking on any of the first four and are instead focusing on the last four!

It would be even better for you if you could be doing more than one of the last four ways to increase your wealth.

Go ahead and write it down – how do you plan to increase your wealth? How are you going to become financially free? No need to get into the detail just now, just broadly speaking what is your strategy going to be? We all want to have more money, right?

As just about all of us know, it is never as simple as we would like it to be and many of us are unable to increase our income significantly over the years. But there are ways to increase income over time, particularly if you run your own business, and it is equally as important if you are helping others run a business. The methods and strategies can apply to both the business owner and the employee.

So, what can be done to increase income? There are clearly a few ways to do this, one of which you could use, but hopefully you could use a combination of all of them.

7 How do I begin to work out what my number is?

Success is the progressive realisation of a worthy goal or ideal

— Earl Nightingale

We have already talked about splitting up your goals into short-term, medium-term and long-term goals, but now I want to take you into more detail on how to achieve your long-term goals and to help you work out **'what your number is'**.

You may be wondering what I mean by **'what your number is'**. This is the amount of money you will need to live the life that you would choose to live today, if you had everything in place that you needed.

When it comes to knowing your number and having 'enough' money to live for the rest of your life without the risk of running out of money, there are four different types of people, and all of us are in one of these categories already.

> **There are the 'haven't got enough' camp,**
>
> **the 'have got just the right amount' camp,**
>
> **the 'have got more than enough' camp,**
>
> **and the 'have more than enough and still want more' camp.**

The chances are that most people will not be in the last two categories unless they are very fortunate. The vast majority of people are probably in one of the first two categories. The problem is that if you do not know your number, you may not know quite what situation you are in. You'd be surprised how many people are well on their way to financial freedom but do not know it yet.

But if you had achieved financial freedom or were on target to achieve it, how would you know? And, more to the point, if you thought you were on target but were going to fall short, imagine how bad you would feel if you had once upon a time had the chance to do something about it. My guess is that you would not be very happy.

Knowing what your number is can be calculated using three factors.

Firstly, **'where do you want to get to?'**

So, taking your long-term list of goals you created earlier, we should consider expanding this and breaking it into further subsections to build a more specific picture of what you want your future to look like.

These sections could include the following:

1. How much money would you need if you were to stop working and earning a salary today?

2. Where would you be living?

3. What future spending would you need now that you are retired?

4. Do you want to leave a legacy to your family or a charity?

Can you see that we are now starting to build a much clearer picture of what you would like your life to be like?

Now that you have established what it is that you want to achieve, the second step is to decide on when you want to achieve this by. Even though this is a long-term goal, your goals may not occur all at the same time. For example, you may wish to have retired from conventional work at age sixty-five and want to move to a new home by the time you reach the age of seventy. And in the middle of all of that, you may have a fabulous world cruise planned. We need to build our future plans around what we want to do or achieve and put a date on when we want those plans to come to fruition.

The final piece of this part of the jigsaw is to establish clearly what strategies we are going to use to help us achieve these goals.

I am assuming that you will already have decided that the first four ways to increase your wealth are not on the list. Just to remind us all, these are **marry it, steal it, inherit it** and **win it**.

So, which of the main and legitimate strategies should you be considering? And should you be working towards more than one of them? We should have more than one strategy and preferably three if possible.

It's not really a secret, but hardly anyone puts it this way. Just about every successful person that has ever lived is also really good at their 'Plan B'. What I mean by that is, right now you will be either working for a company or running your own business, but the savvy financial freedom planners are also doing something else with some of their money. This is particularly the case for business owners, who may have plans to sell their business in the future but recognise that it doesn't always work out like that. The truth of selling a business is that most businesses never get sold as the owner *is* the business. Even if the business does get sold, it is rarely for what the business owners think that it is worth.

Having a really solid 'Plan B' for most of us is essential, so we all need to get really good at our 'Plan B', whatever it may be. To remind us all, our options are **property investing, stocks & shares** and **selling our intellectual property.** It's up to you to decide which path will work best for you.

What we all need to consider is the risks each one of these exposes us to and how much risk we as individuals are prepared to take on ourselves. We are all different and have different tolerance levels which we can live with on a day-to-day basis. The golden rule is, 'if it keeps you awake at night, you are taking too much risk'.

To summarise, we all need to clearly establish the following goals to start putting our financial freedom plan together.

1. **Where do I want to get to?**

2. **When do I want to get there by?**

3. **What am I going to do to get there?**

In the wise words of Alan Lakein: 'Planning is bringing the future into the present, so that we can do something about it now.'

8 Looking after number one

Money is like a teenager, it thinks it can look after itself

— Unknown

We could fall into a fatal trap, a trap that literally millions of people fall into every day, every week, every month, year after year. This trap leads to all sorts of troubles and not all are financial problems; in fact, relationship difficulties being top of the list.

What I am talking about is **'running out of money before running out of month or week'**, depending upon how often you are paid or how often you pay yourself if you run your own business. And it is not a problem that just besets those that don't earn enough money. We can all be forgiven for thinking that if we earned just a bit more money then everything would be okay. Unfortunately, we all have demands on the money that we make, and for many of us it is often just not quite enough to do what we want to do. Quite often, if you we earn a bit more money, your partner's and children's needs are first in the queue. And even if your family are not in need of your extra income, the chances are that you may need to spend it on something for yourself or on your house. We all know the picture, right?

Those famous last words, 'If I earned a bit more money, I will be okay', are just not going to work and we know it. Can you remember how much you were earning ten years ago? My guess is that you are probably earning more today, but you never seem to be any better off. Sound familiar?

The traditional view that many people take is that they will save whatever is left at the end of the month! But as we all know, there is never any left. With modern banking apps, we can see how much is in our bank account every minute of every day and this causes an even bigger problem. Many people are guilty of micro-managing their money on a day-by-day basis, and if they think that there may be some surplus then there is the tendency to spend more money, when we should be doing something else with it.

So, what is the answer to this problem?

The answer is very simple: we MUST pay ourselves first. As money comes into our personal bank account through our wages, salary or however we get paid, we need to deal with it straight away, so that it can do different jobs for us. So whatever amount we need to be saving each month absolutely MUST leave our personal bank account as soon as we are paid. Many people only have one bank account, but with modern banking we can all have multiple accounts that we can view at any time and that we can use for different jobs. We should have a 'bills' account and everything else should be directed to another account, which could be your savings account, your holiday account or whatever it needs to be. Have you ever heard of a friend who pays for their annual holiday on their credit card and then spends the rest of the year paying it off? This must be avoided at all costs.

So, the minute your income hits your account, how much you need for your non-bills expenditure needs to leave your account, either into another account or to some form of investment account or wherever it needs to go. This is just good personal financial management, and even if you do nothing else the personal management of your money will improve dramatically. Not only is it good housekeeping, but it brings added discipline to the management of your money, which helps you become more enthusiastic about reaching for your financial goals and aspirations.

Our job, to summarise, is to save/invest before we start spending. Spending is fun, I know, but we must have the foundations built first. After doing this for a few months, you will soon find that you are living on the reduced amount of income, because you have put a disciplined solution in place. If you have not started doing this already, it's great fun to see your asset base getting bigger every month. And if things go wrong for some reason, you will have money saved that can get you out of that hole. Hopefully, you won't need it, but having a backup fund is comforting and helps us all sleep better at night.

9 15% is the new rule and that's just to start

If you don't know where you are going, any road will take you there

– Lewis Carroll

There is one question that I get asked all the time. The problem with the question is that in a brief conversation it is virtually impossible to answer, but everyone wants to know the answer. The trouble is, even if we calculate what the answer to the question is, most people don't like the answer. Sometimes the truth can be a bitter pill to swallow, but we all very much need to get used to the idea if we want to achieve our goals of financial freedom.

There is a problem with the question, especially from a financial planning perspective, as there are just far too many variables to answer it and it is different for everyone. Without doing some serious calculations, taking into account where you are now and where you want to get to, it's very difficult to answer quickly.

So, what question am I talking about?

The question is, **'How much do I need to invest so that I can retire?'**

The answer to the question is almost **'How long is a piece of string?'**

Even though it is a difficult question to answer, that does not mean it cannot be calculated, but we do need a starting point.

Many of us will already be contributing to some form of retirement account especially if we are employed as all companies, certainly in the United Kingdom, are legally obliged to enrol their qualifying employees into a workplace pension scheme. Not all employees have to be enrolled if they are below a certain age or over a certain age. There is however an enormous problem with these types of retirement accounts and that is that the contribution levels are woefully low and well below what really needs to be invested to build up a meaningful retirement fund.

Currently, the self-employed are not required by law to invest into a retirement account and as such many self-employed people do not contribute on a regular basis to this type of arrangement. Many of them are either relying on the sale of their business or are doing something else to create their own financial freedom. Sadly, some are doing nothing at all. For those who plan to sell a business, this is a risky strategy – but more on that later.

So, if the amount that is being invested into a retirement account is far too low, the logical question is, **'How much should it be?'**

First of all, let's look at what the current funding levels are likely to achieve. If the current rate of investing into a retirement account is 5% of your income, that in simple terms means, that it will take you twenty years to have invested just one year's worth of income! That is scary.

If a typical working life is forty years, in simple terms only 5 or 10% of your income has been put towards creating a secure financial future, there is a strong possibility that there will be a problem in the future. It doesn't take too long to work out that this is not going to work. Of course, there is investment returns to be taken into account, but even exceptional investment returns are not going to make enough difference to create financial freedom.

If the typical retirement age is in a person's mid-sixties and they live on average for twenty to twenty-five years in retirement, there needs to be a different approach.

Everyone's situation is different, especially as we are all starting from different places and have different timescales, but we need to have a starting point from which to begin, if we are going to be serious about achieving financial freedom.

As a minimum, we should be saving/investing for our future at least 15% of our annual income every year and we should begin as soon as we start to earn. If you are still living at home with your parents, the amount should be considerably more as you will probably want to buy your own home at some point in the future.

Depending on your current situation, some of this money should be invested into an account to build a deposit for your first home and for others that are closer to the time when they will stop working, this should be targeted at your plans for the time when you stop working and retire.

When I suggest to people that they should be investing 15% of their income every year, many of them tell me that they couldn't possibly afford to save that much as they need as much of their income as possible to live from month to month. My advice here is that we all must look at where our money is going and identify what it is being spent on, so that we can get serious about building a secure financial future. In simple terms, there may need to be some short-term pains (i.e. getting used to having less spendable income), so that we can enjoy some long-term gains.

For some of us who are late in starting our financial future plans, the amount may need to be even more, but at least 15% is a significant start. And once you have started and can see the amounts start to increase quite quickly, the chances are that you will become more enthusiastic about achieving your goals and aspirations.

I recently watched a film called *Hell or High Water* – not a great film, but it had one memorable line for me: **'*Poorness is like a disease, passing from generation to generation.*'**

Breaking the cycle not only helps us now, but also can help lay the foundation for our own children and grandchildren. Creating the habits of not spending everything and planning for a better, more secure financial future is not necessarily just for ourselves and our immediate family right now. It can be the launchpad to improve our family's lives for generations to come.

The takeaway: Start by saving 15% of your income each month as soon as you get paid.

10 Every kind of money you will ever need

Money isn't everything, but I'd like to try it out for myself first

– Unknown

What do we need money for? To live, of course, but it is not the daft question that it looks like at first. The real question is, what are the different things that we need money for? What jobs do we need money to do for us? We often hear that the wise man says we only need money to put a roof over our heads and food on the table, and of course he is right. But if we are to become financially free, knowing the different jobs or tasks that we need money for will most definitely help us create and execute a plan to get us there.

Every kind of money that we could ever need can be put into six different categories. Unfortunately, the 80% that do not reach at least some kind of financial freedom never get to the point where they have the opportunity to create enough wealth to be able to have the six different types of money.

So, what are the six different types of money?

The first type of money we need is **'survival money'**. There are only three essential needs in life. We need shelter, food and water. Everything else is a bonus. If this was all that we needed or wanted, the amount required for most of us is not really a great deal. This really is the minimum amount each of us needs just to survive. It goes without saying that having only this amount of money is a huge risk.

The second type of money we need is **'essential outgoing money'**. This type of money is beyond 'survival money' but is still really important in order to at least live a relatively comfortable life. This is the money we need to keep a comfortable home, money to put more than just basic food on the table. Money to cover the type of monthly expenditure which in the truest sense is not really absolutely essential but most of us would consider to be up there as being important. Most people who live in Western society have this covered, fortunately.

The third type of money we need is what I call **'get out of jail money'**. It is not literally get out of jail money, of course, but rather this is the money you need to solve a financial problem that is not part of your regular financial outgoings on a month-by-month basis. This is an expenditure that comes along out of the blue that just cannot be avoided. It just has to be paid. An example of this might be having to replace your boiler, or unexpected repair work to your car. It is kind of essential, but you have not budgeted for it on a monthly basis. Sadly, many people do not have this base covered and therefore could literally be one month's pay cheque away from financial catastrophe.

The fourth type of money we need is **'comfortable life money'**. This is the sort of money that allows you to live a life of more comfort. Money that allows you to enjoy a few extras in life. Money that allows you to eat out a few times a month or each week. Money that allows you to have a few holidays a year. This is money that starts to make you feel like all the savings you made over the years, all the sacrifices you made were all worthwhile. Your plan, after all, made a difference to you and those around you.

The fifth type of money is the **'serious fun money'**. We all know someone who has this type of money, but there are not that many of them. These people have often been very successful in planning their finances for retirement. They most definitely had a plan and it worked. This sort of money allows you to be generous with your friends and family, it allows you to have those special holidays that we all dream of and eat in those extra special restaurants.

The sixth and final type of money is what I call **'legacy money'**. Let's face it, most of us want to leave a legacy to our children and our grandchildren. It's human nature to want to give the next generation a good start in life and for them to surpass what we have achieved. Lots of people try and do this before they have secured their own future, foregoing the life that they really deserve for their children and grandchildren. But, imagine how you would feel if you could not only live the life you want and deserve *and* be able to leave a legacy of some meaning. To be remembered for future generations is the greatest legacy one can leave.

11 How to increase your income

*When you do more than you get paid for,
eventually you'll be paid for more
than you do*

– Zig Ziglar

To fill our buckets of wealth up, it's probably a good idea to consider all possible options to make sure that our income is as high as it really could be. To give ourselves the best possible opportunity to become financially free, earning more money is certainly going to help. So, any strategies that are going to help us here are very important. And it goes without saying, all of the ideas here assume that that you use them in a legal way, a moral way and a compliant way. I am not talking about doing anything that is unethical or may harm other people.

Whether you are running your own business or working for someone else, the reality is that there are really only four ways to increase your income. There are only four ways to have more money in your pocket that you can use to invest in yourself. In fact, this is so important. Before I go any further, you must get into the habit of paying yourself first. It is the most important rule of becoming financially free.

At the very highest level there are only four ways to increase the amount of money that you have. Don't worry if you are employed and are working for someone else – this information is just as important to you. If you help the owner of the business you work for make more money, sooner or later they will pay you more, because they will want to keep you as you will be a valuable part of the team.

So, what are the ways to increase the amount of money earned?

1. Reduce costs. The first way to make money is to reduce or lower costs. If you are the business owner or work for one, a reduction in overheads will mean you have more money in the bank account at the end of every month. More money will mean greater choices and more options. So, every opportunity to save money should be considered and this exercise should be reviewed regularly. Taking the same approach to your personal finances is just as important. A great way to do this is to use a spreadsheet to analyse what your income is being spent on each month. Unfortunately, most people don't know exactly where their money is going. You may be surprised when you carry out the exercise and identify where your money is going. You will be amazed how much money just disappears in what I call 'leakage'. The essential bills will make up a good proportion of your costs, but there is also likely to be an additional amount of money that just gets spent somewhere, every month.

If you can identify how much this is and reduce it as much as possible, you've just found some extra money that can be put towards your financial freedom plan.

2. Increase prices. The second way to increase the amount of money you have available is to increase your prices. Now, this is not always as easy as you would hope, as many businesses are competing on price. In my opinion a business competing on price is going to end up with a competitor undercutting them sooner or later. We all have experience of a competitor tendering for work that is below our own break-even point. This is a situation where one of your competitors is buying business in the hope that they can make a profit in the long run. This is not where you want to be positioning your business.

So, what should you be doing instead? My opinion is that it is essential to differentiate what you do on something other than price. What that differentiation is will depend on what service or product you offer. What is most certainly true is that if you can get away from competing on price, you are in a far better position to charge more for what you offer. If your offering or service is good enough, different enough, there is a fair chance that you will be able to charge your customers more.

3. Diversify. The third way to increase your income is to increase your offering. What are the things your customers need that are associated with what you do and that you are not offering now? Diversification could be in the form of similar products or services, or even complimentary products. In simple terms, if you are offering a product you could also be supplying the tools to fit your product.

Another way to diversify is to consider offering services or products up or down the supply chain. Again, if you supply a product, you can also be offering a service to fit the product, which of course you can charge a fee for.

4. Sell more. Finally, the last option to increase your income is to sell more of what you do. Now, you might say that you cannot sell more because you are already working very hard. However, to sell more, could you bring in another member of your team that can help you sell more of your product or service? Who can you bring in to your team, that will free up your time to be able to sell more of your product or service? I often find that many people are working on far too many tasks at any given time and as such they are not getting the very best from themselves.

If you can focus on just three or four tasks and ensure that someone else is doing all the other tasks, you massively increase your chances of being able to sell more of your product or service.

All this may sound like it is only relevant to a business owner, but don't dismiss the ideas if you work for someone else. If as an employee you can help the business owner in these four key areas, I can assure you that your efforts will be noticed and if you are working for a good company you will eventually be rewarded. If this does not happen, maybe it is time to consider a move. I have found that people who are unappreciated and unrewarded may even have to start the process to move only to find at the last moment that the business will realise that you are too valuable to lose and will pay you more. So, yes, this section is just as relevant to employees as business owners.

I have included a template in Appendix 2 to help you with ideas on how to increase your income.

12 How to control leakage

No pain, no gain

– Jane Fonda

The biggest problem that I hear week in, week out is this: 'I can't afford to save for the future right now. I don't earn enough as it is.'

Sound familiar? I am sure that it does, because so many people are either in that place or have been. Another reason I hear for not saving goes something like this.

'If I just earned another £5,000 a year or £10,000 a year, then I'll be able to start.'

I am guessing that you've heard that one before, and even said it yourself as well.

I'll let you into a secret. An increase in your income is unlikely to make little if any difference, and here's why. Without a shift in our mindset any increase in our income is unlikely to make much of a difference, unless your income goes up by an unfathomable amount, such as a 100% increase. And the single biggest reason is that most people live according to their means. Huge numbers of people run out of money before they run out of month. Money just leaks away; sound familiar?

Have you ever calculated how much your monthly bills add up to and thought, 'Well, there's plenty to spare for me to save', and then get to the end of the month and there is nothing left? If this is you, you are absolutely not alone.

That is because there is a huge possibility of leakage. What I mean by leakage is spending that just doesn't fit in the regular expenditure boxes. This is not the electricity or the gas bills, not the council tax. It's something else much more challenging to identify. I can give you a few clues though. It could be your favourite coffee that you pick up on the way to work every day, the Friday night drinks you have after work, how much you spend on meals out. Believe me, it all adds up to quite a chunk of money.

Why do some people get it wrong?

The problem for a lot of people is that their financial freedom plan is based on saving what is 'left over' at the end of the month. And there rarely is any. Can you see the problem? I bet you can.

So, what is the answer?

The answer is to work on your financial freedom plan at the beginning of the month or as soon as you get paid and not to wait for the end of the month to see what is left. The golden rule is to pay yourself first – this is your savings/investments money – and use the rest of your income to live on. Now most people say, 'That's just impossible – I can't survive on what I get now.'

I beg to differ. Can you remember just a few years ago – you were probably earning less than you are now and you survived perfectly well then. If we follow two simple rules, we can get our financial freedom plan underway very quickly.

Firstly, next time you get a pay rise, instead of absorbing this into your usual living expenditure, start to save this extra money immediately.

Secondly – and this is really important and the key to your success – instead of waiting until the end of the month to see what is left, pay money into your savings in a separate account immediately after you get paid. No delaying, no hesitation, pay into your savings straight away. Earlier in this book I suggested at least 10 to 15% of your income should be saved and ideally this is where you should start.

You may think that this is just impossible. But is it? I have been there myself and I can tell you that after a few months you get used to the new level of income, and the new level of income becomes the norm. Yes, it is a little painful to start with, but you will soon get used to it. As painful as it is to start with, it is worthwhile in order to get to where you want to. The other thing about saving this way, is that it is a great habit too. In no time at all, you could be saving 15% a month. This savings thing can become addictive, not to mention very rewarding.

One other massive leakage I come across quite often is the cost of holidays and how they are paid for. I often come across people who put the cost of their annual holiday on a credit card and spend the next nine months paying it off at huge rates of interest. This is just about the worst way to pay for a holiday. All that money that you are paying in interest could be going towards saving for your financial freedom day.

It is far better to save in advance for a holiday in a separate account rather than pay for it afterwards. Now, this does require some forward planning, but it is essential if you wish to avoid painful interest payments on a purchase that has been and gone months ago. Set up a separate holiday savings account to make this easier for you to manage.

Leakage control is so important and often overlooked by many people, which either temporarily or permanently delays their future financial plans.

13 Staying true to the cause

Rome was not built in a day, but they were laying bricks every hour

— John Heywood

The problem with planning for a great financial future is that unfortunately it does take time, unless you have an absolutely fantastic idea that catapults your wealth rapidly. The road to financial freedom is littered with people who have lost their way and given up.

Most people massively overestimate what they can achieve over the short term, but massively underestimate what can be achieved over the long term. That is such an important point that I want you to read it again and take some time to absorb the full meaning of it. It really is one of the foundations of success, whether it is about creating financial freedom, running a marathon, or anything else in life for that matter.

The key to success is to stay completely focused, to stay on track and not be derailed. Believe me, it is very easy to become disheartened and your plans can easily fall by the wayside.

So, why is it that we can become distracted from the job in hand? It's quite simple, really. If you consider how life is for just about everyone, it goes something like this:

Most days involve dealing with problem-solving. Most of the time we just go from one problem-solving issue to another and then every now and then a major problem/disaster occurs which we have to solve. And most of the time, we solve these problems because that is the way life is. So, if you were thinking that you were the only one who had all these issues, you are far from alone. From those just starting out on their financial freedom journey to those who have created significant wealth, they are all following a similar path.

If you are struggling to put together a plan for your financial future, the chances are that you are getting distracted from getting to your end goal. This is because we can generally cope with the problem-solving day in day out that most people do every day. However, the problems often arise when one of these disasters/crises occurs and we must look at what we are doing. Sometimes it is necessary to put our lives on hold to sort out the problems.

Dealing with these minor disasters is what we must do, and most people move on from them. However, quite often there are a number of after-effects that can be a major problem on the route to financial freedom.

Firstly, after suffering a setback many people never get back on track and start to rebuild their future plan. If that happens, the chances of achieving financial freedom are drastically reduced or, at the very least, delayed.

Secondly, for those that do re-start their financial freedom plan, their confidence can be utterly shattered and what they do instead is choose a much more cautious path that will ultimately mean that it will take a great deal longer to get to the end of their journey.

This is a perfectly natural human reaction, but it is not necessarily the most appropriate course of action. After suffering a setback, despite the natural urge to be very cautious, it is important to still look at the long-term picture and, if it is still appropriate, some level of risk still has to be accepted. Being ultra-cautious all of your life is not going to help you.

Let me give you an example. If you were to suffer a major setback but you still had twenty years before retirement, taking a cautious approach from now onwards is not going to be in your best interest. What many people do in this instance is convince themselves that risk is not for them and hold all their savings in deposit accounts. Of course, this money is earning very little and more than likely going backwards in real terms as inflation erodes the value.

Of course, it is important to have money held on deposit, but long-term money will work much better for you if it is invested in an investment that will give you the chance for it to grow in real terms ahead of inflation.

In summary, after a major setback, try to avoid becoming overly cautious and always remember that it is the long-term result that really is the most important.

14 Compound interest – the double-edged sword

Compound interest is the eighth wonder of the world. He who understands it, earns it. He who doesn't … pays it

– Albert Einstein

If you had to choose between being given £1 million today or one penny today and that amount doubles every day for the next thirty days, which would you choose. The instant answer for most people is the £1 million.

That's a lot of money, yes? **But is taking the million the right choice?**

So, how could one pence doubling every day ever be anywhere near £1 million? Without doubt most people would prefer the £1 million today, but they would definitely have made the wrong choice. The second option of one penny doubling every day would give you £5,368,709.12 after thirty days. Yes, you did read that correctly. You would have £5,368,709.12 in your bank account after 30 days. That is the incredible power of compound interest so, as you can see, it really should not be underestimated. Now, obviously, it is totally unreasonable to expect your money to double every day or even every year but is does demonstrate how powerful compound interest is. The problem with compound interest, though, is that it is pretty dull and uninteresting for quite a while. And here's why. Let's look at the numbers.

Day 1	**£0.01**
Day 2	£0.02
Day 3	£0.04
Day 4	£0.08
Day 5	£0.16

As you can see, the numbers are not that interesting to start with and new investors can, and often do, become disillusioned. The end result is that they give up before it has even really started. Given the early day results, those that are not fully bought into the desire to become financially free will, and do, find it very easy to give up. Very simply, this is why a great number of people end up at the end of their working lives with insufficient savings and investments to support them in the life of comfort they had hoped for just a few decades before. All is not lost, however. Let's look at the numbers if you had stayed committed and kept saving and investing over the long term. The numbers now look a great deal more interesting.

Day 26	£335,544.32
Day 27	£671,088.64
Day 28	£1,342,177.28
Day 29	£2,684,354.56
Day 30	£5,368,709.12

As you can see, the numbers now look a lot more interesting. So, if you knew that your savings would behave in a similar way, albeit at a different rate of return, you may well be far more interested in continuing in your investment program for a secure financial future. It can be summed up in the following analogy:

> *'To become an overnight success,*
> *it takes ten years of hard work.'*

In this case it is longer than ten years, but I am sure you can see the point that I am making. Whilst others are giving up, those that strive to continue will eventually reap the rewards and will achieve the nirvana of financial freedom.

On the flip side of EARNING compound interest is having to pay compounding interest. Even in these days of low interest rates, over a typical mortgage payment period of twenty-five years, it is almost inevitable that interest rates will go through periods of being very low, as they are today, to being extremely high at some point. It is not all that long ago that the standard mortgage rate was 15%. Can you imagine the problems caused for most people if the rates returned to those levels? All I can say on that subject is if it happened before it can happen again. 'It's different this time' is quite possibly the most dangerous mindset of all.

Even though most of us have to accept that we will need to borrow money to buy a house at the very least, becoming debt-free should be a priority, even if interest rates are very low and you believe that they will remain so for the long term. If you are still not convinced, ask your mortgage company to provide you with a statement of how much you will pay in interest over the term of your mortgage, assuming the current interest rate. It will run into the tens of thousands of pounds. This is the 'compound interest' being earning by your mortgage company and money that you will never see. It is the price we have to pay to have a mortgage to buy a home.

So, what should we do?

The simple answer is, wherever possible, we should pay down the mortgage debt as quickly as possible, either through monthly overpayments or one-off payments, provided the mortgage lender will allow this. There is something deeply satisfying about being mortgage free as quickly as possible. Being mortgage-free gives us a great deal more choices than we would otherwise have had.

In summary, it is essential to give money time to do its job. Be patient and stick to the plan and you will benefit from the power of interest/growth over the long term. In the end, money begets money.

And secondly, do not let cheap money convince you to stay in debt for longer than you have to be. The mortgage lenders would love you to do this, but it is not really in your best interest, certainly over the long term.

15 Diversification

History shows you don't know what the
future brings

                                      – Richard Wagoner

I get asked this question all of the time, and it is the wrong question.

'Where's the best place to invest right now?'

I get asked this question just about everywhere I go if people know that I am
a financial planner. There is a major problem with this question in that I just
don't know anywhere near enough about that person's situation, in terms of
their timescale or how much risk they can live with, just to mention a few
factors.

So why is diversification so important?

Investors all over the world develop habits that might work out but very
often cause them major problems. Do you remember your mum saying to
you, 'Don't put all your eggs in one basket'? Yes, we all known that one very
well, but what do investors do? Put all their eggs in one basket. Here are a
few examples.

Property investors are often blind to any other type of investing and will not
even consider whether investing in other assets have any merit. Unbeliev-
ably, I have been asked to facilitate the withdrawal of pension fund money
from defined benefit pension schemes to invest in buy-to-let property. For
those that don't know, a defined benefit pension (sometimes known as a
final salary pension) has guaranteed benefits and in most cases should not

be given up lightly. Property can be addictive, and many investors try to buy more and more of the same thing.

Some stocks-and-shares investors only invest in one sector or even just one fund. That is very much putting all of your eggs into one basket.

The problem with one strategy is this. No one – and I mean absolutely no one – knows what type of investment, whether that be property, or stocks and shares, will be the most profitable investment to hold for the long term.

Even if you were supremely confident, as many are (why else would you invest in the first place?), why would you take the risk of investing in just one type of investment? All sorts of problems can occur that can have a seriously detrimental effect on your financial position. Here are a few to consider.

- The global economy moves into recession.

- The government changes the law and makes an investment unattractive.

- Your investment type may become illiquid (i.e. no buyers when you need to sell).

As you can see, being in one type of investment can lead to all sorts of problems. This can be a particularly difficult problem, especially for property investors. This type of investment is usually quite illiquid at the best of times and in difficult times it can be extremely difficult to dispose of. This is not to say that you should not be considering property in your overall investment portfolio as it can be very effective. The problem is this: If all of your money is invested in property and you have to raise money quickly, you could have a big problem on your hands.

Similarly, if all of your money is invested in one share or fund, when the markets are falling you have few options, other than to suffer a loss of value on disposal. The only advantage is that at least you can sell your investment, as there is always a market for shares. In extreme circumstances even, this option evaporates if the shares are suspended for one reason or another. It is then impossible to withdraw funds even if you wanted to.

Going back to the original question that I get asked all of the time – 'Where's the best place to invest right now?' The very simple answer to that question is that there is no best place, and even if there was, it would be a different answer for everyone as we all have different time scales, different risk tolerances and most definitely different objectives. Before deciding on where to invest, finding the answer to those questions is essential.

In any case, if you do come across someone that claims to be able to tell you the best place to invest or has a great investment idea that is GUARANTEED to make you a great return, there is one thing that you must do. That is *run away as fast as you can* as quick as you can.

These types of people are either charlatans or have no idea what they are talking about. They certainly do not have the requisite qualifications to be able to advise or guide anyone.

If there isn't one best place to invest your money, what is the **best *way* to invest your money?**

Short-term money needs should be held in quickly, if not immediately, accessible savings/deposit accounts. Even though these types of accounts earn little or no interest, it is more important the money can be accessed quickly and when required.

Medium- and long-term money requires a different approach. Spreading where you invest is essential if you are to avoid some of the problems I have mentioned above. For example, if property is your chosen investment, buying property of all one type or all in one area is a high-risk strategy. Buying different types of property and also at different price points is a more balanced approach and gives you more options in the future. For example, over the last ten years or so, multi-let properties have proven to be very popular. The sector is now facing significant problems as legislative changes have had a negative impact.

If conventional investing in stocks and share type investments is your preference, once again a diversified portfolio – across not only a number of funds but also across a number of sectors – is essential. If all of your money is investment in one fund, in the UK stock market, sooner or later the value is going to be affected adversely. It is far more prudent to invest in a broad spread of investments, as the reality is that no one person knows for sure what sectors or what funds are going to perform the best.

The name of the game is to spread the risk.

As a homeowner, you are already invested in property, so in the interest of taking a diversified strategy to achieving financial freedom, stocks and share type investments offer a more balanced approach. Even professional landlords would be wise to consider diversifying into other types of investments.

In summary, holding all your eggs in one basket may just work, but there is far too much risk for most of us to bear with this strategy. Diversify your investment portfolio across a range of investments or else you will be increasing your overall risk dramatically.

16 Good debt, bad debt

A man who pays his bills on time is soon forgotten
— Oscar Wilde

'If you haven't got the money to buy it, you can't have it.' We've all heard that before or something very similar. However much you believe this to be true, it is only a truism up to a point. There are certainly two types of debt: debt that will sink you and debt that helps you. Used correctly, debt will help improve your wealth or at the very least help you acquire assets that will increase in value over time.

It goes without saying that some debt should be avoided at all costs or, if this is not possible, restricted to an absolute minimum and for as short a period of time as possible.

Probably the most dangerous debt that modern society faces is credit card debt. Credit card debt often paralyses a person's ability to achieve financial freedom and sadly many people are never able to escape this type of debt as it can quite easily get to the point where the interest payments are all that some people can afford to pay each month. Credit card debt is so dangerous because it is far too easy to get and secondly, this being the real 'killer', the interest rates are crushingly high. Interest rates of more than 20% or sometimes in excess of 30% will rapidly destroy your ability to repay the debt and almost certainly prevent you from growing your wealth.

But if you find yourself in a situation where using a credit card is absolutely essential, make sure you do it in the most effective way, which involves just two rules. Rule number 1: Always pay off the debt in FULL each month. And the second rule: Never, ever forget rule number 1!

Credit cards can be very effective and a useful way to manage your money, but you must be in control. The minute you let your credit card take control, you are onto a loser and it becomes very difficult to get out of it. Not to mention that it is painful to climb out of that hole. Credit cards do have their place in financial management for sure and can be very effective in building up your credit score, but you must be careful with their use.

So what kind of debt is 'good' debt?

Debt that you use to acquire an asset that is likely to appreciate in value. For most of us, we need to borrow money to purchase our homes and the mortgages that we take out would be regarded by most people as good debt. Whilst there is no certainty that the value of our home will increase in value, history has shown that the values do increase over time. There are often periods when house prices do not go up and on occasions even fall in value. However, over the longer term, the values increase. It is important to remember however, that we should not necessarily regard our homes as an investment.

The other aspect that makes a mortgage a 'good debt' is that the interest rates are much, much lower than credit card interest rates and most people will now use some form of fixed rate to ensure that they know what the monthly outgoing will be for a period of time. Rates can be fixed for anything from one year to ten years. What option you choose will depend upon your personal circumstances and your future plans.

What should you do if you have both a mortgage and credit card debt?

Firstly, they will all have to be paid off eventually. However, the priority when it comes to paying off debt is to pay off the most expensive debt first and then focus on the lower cost debt. So, if you have credit card debt, work on clearing this before your mortgage. Unlike many, do not be tempted to convert credit card debt in to mortgage debt. Even though mortgage interest rates are much lower than credit card interest rates, converting credit card debt into a twenty-five-year loan via your mortgage will almost certainly cost you more in the long run.

Painful as it may be, the short-term pain of paying off credit card debt is much better for your long-term financial freedom. And don't delay – many people put their head in the sand over credit card debt and the issue can become insurmountable. It is essential to get a grip of the problem before it becomes overwhelming.

In summary, expensive debt can and will wipe you out permanently. On the other hand, controlled long-term debt that is within your means can help you create valuable assets that will ultimately form part of your financial plan. Be one of those people who uses debt to help build their lives and not make life more difficult than it needs to be. As Oscar Wilde suggests, you will be forgotten if you pay your debts off, but if you don't, the loan provider will soon come looking for you and life will become unbearably uncomfortable.

17 Creating a cashflow model

Planning is bringing the future into the present so that you can do something about it

— Alan Lakein

If you've ever worked in any kind of business or run your own, you are sure to have come across the 'cashflow model'. Just about every business owner will have either created a cashflow model for the future or will be running one right now. No business owner would start out without some form of plan as to how the business might grow, to cover the costs and to make a profit. That much you can be sure of.

In business, if you don't know where you are headed, there is a fair chance that you will have no idea when you will get there, if at all.

But how many times do you hear people talking about their own personal cashflow model? Almost never! But you really should be doing it, and here's why.

People often ask me this question; in fact, it happens nearly every week.

'How much money do I need saved up to retire?'

'How much income do you need?' is the response I usually give. If you know how much you need, we can work out what needs to be done to get to where you want to get to. The way to do this is build a model of what your future years may look like and the build-up of your assets to create your own financial freedom.

So, how do I create a cashflow model for myself?

First of all, you need to start with where you are now. What have you already accumulated, what are you able to comfortably afford to save now, and where do you want to get to in the future? Using this information, you can begin to put together a schedule of how your asset base may begin to build up over time. It is important to factor in investment returns, inflation and also how your ability to save for the future will increase over time as your income increases.

After putting together a model like this, there are three potential outcomes:

1. You will get there sooner than you think – very exciting!

2. You may never get there at all on your current plans – very scary.

3. Or, it all comes together just at the right time for you and your family – happy days.

When many people put together a projection/cashflow model for their future, the results are often scary and disappointing, which can be tremendously off-putting. But don't be deterred. What most people are not factoring in is that they will more than likely earn more in the future and, as a consequence, will be able to save more.

The really smart cookies use their increased income to accelerate the repayment of personal mortgages and other debts, freeing up more disposable income to increase their savings sooner rather than later. Get this bit right and guess what, you may end up being in the first category above. Now, wouldn't that be nice? There is nothing more satisfying than making the final payment on your mortgage and having a healthy balance of savings and investments. It is really quite liberating knowing that no one can come after you for more money going forward. It's not quite winning the lottery, not that you should be playing it anyway, but nevertheless it's very satisfying.

In summary, know where you are now, know where you want to get to, but not just in your head. Commit your plan to paper and keep working on your personal cashflow plan. A written down plan is far better than hoping for the best in our head.

18 Celebrate your success

Giving credit where credit is due is a very reward-ing habit to form

– Loretta Young

The problem with long-term plans is that they are just too difficult to maintain your interest in – just too boring for most of us. So, the big question here is how do we get over this and keep on track?

First of all, it is important to understand the context that leads us to the struggle of maintaining our motivation.

Ask yourself this question: 'Do I want to enjoy "things" in life now or would I prefer to wait and enjoy these "things" later in life?' If you are like most people, you want to enjoy things now rather than later. Notice how I didn't use the word 'spend', but doing 'things' now and 'spending', in this context, are one and the same thing. 'Things' cost money.

Planning for the future is exclusively about deferring things we could do now in favour of things that we would like to do later. And I can tell you, that it is not easy for any of us. To put this into context, allow me to tell you a little story.

A small group of children were put into an enclosed room at a table and in front of them each was placed a single marshmallow. They were instructed that they had two choices. They could eat the marshmallow at any time over the next fifteen minutes if they wished. However, if they waited the full fifteen minutes they would be given another marshmallow.

What do you think happened?

I can tell you that almost all of the children could not resist and ate the marshmallow straight away or at some point before the fifteen minutes was up. Very few of the children were able to resist eating the sweet, even though they knew that they could have another one if they waited. It is absolutely human nature to consume (enjoy) now rather than defer the pleasure for later. Humans are hard-wired this way.

What became even more interesting about this story is that a number of years later the children where once again observed as adults. The results of the survey were very interesting indeed. The children that were able to resist the longest as children were found to be more successful and many areas of their lives, in terms of careers and financial success. Isn't that a remarkable finding? After all, who can resist a marshmallow?

So, how can we learn to resist the metaphorical marshmallow?

My belief is that we can't all be grade-A students; we can't all have phenomenal will power to resist the temptations that come along in life daily, weekly, all of the time. So, having a strategy in place that can at the very least give us better chance of not eating the metaphorical marshmallow is going to give us the best possible chance of success. If we have a good strategy, we at the very least are going to do better than those that have no strategy at all.

Setting intermediate goals accompanied by intermediate rewards has long been the best proven way of keeping motivated and on track to our goals. Like running a marathon, just having the goal of completing 26.2 miles will probably get you there ... eventually, as I know all too well. By comparison the athlete who sets intermediate targets is setting themselves up for a better result and greater success. A marathon runner may aim to reach the first 10 miles by a certain time and will reward themselves with not only self-praise, but this may also be the time that they take on extra fuel. And even if they do not achieve the time that they have set for themselves, they still keep on track and continue with the schedule. A marathon runner that has no intermediate goals and rewards could well slip back, lose their motivation, end up walking and could pull out altogether.

On your journey to financial freedom, setting goals and rewards is essential for success for two reasons. Firstly, it keeps you on track to reach your goals, but secondly and most importantly, it always prepares you for the time when you achieve your goals. Have you ever met a financially successful person that seems to have it all, but just can't enjoy their money? Yes, we have all met them and this is usually because they have never stopped to reward themselves on the journey; they've never learnt to appreciate what they have actually achieved.

In summary, setting intermediate targets is not the only target. Accompanying this with rewards on the way, will not only help keep you on track but will also prepare you for the time when you have achieved financial freedom. The rewards do not need to be extravagant, they just need to be something that you would not normally do for yourself or your family on a regular basis. Maybe it is a weekend away or a special something that you have always wanted just for yourself. Success is nearly always accompanied by little goals and rewards on the way.

19 Passive income is a myth

An investment in knowledge pays the best dividends

— Benjamin Franklin

If I have heard it once, I have heard it a thousand times. It goes something like this: 'If you sign up to this program … you too can live like me.' Or perhaps you've heard: 'Invest in this off-plan property investment and secure a passive income …' Blah, blah, blah …

We have all received these kinds of emails, seen the social media ads and even met someone in a bar claiming that they have done this or that and now they are completely retired, when they don't even look like they are old enough to have finished their education.

As much as we would all like it to work out like that, there are just no ideas out there that will give you a life-long passive income. Just about everything you do will, and does, require some work and time to make it happen. If it was the case that you could just generate a passive income out of nowhere, why would anyone tell you how to do it anyway? They would be keeping the secret to themselves whilst sitting on their super yacht in the Caribbean, surely?

So please, don't get drawn into the promise of endless wealth for little or no effort. You will soon be parted from your money and will probably never see the passive income at the very least, and never get your capital back.

What should you avoid?

1. Investments that promise or guarantee double-digit investment returns for life

2. Property investment schemes for off-plan developments guaranteeing occupancy

3. Automated currency trading investments

These are just a few of the scams that are continually promoted to unsuspecting investors. And they keep being pushed on the unsuspecting, because people keep buying them. Fool's gold comes to mind.

If it sounds too good to be true, it most certainly will be too good to be true.

It is essential that you avoid these types of investments at all costs, or you will set your financial freedom plan back for what could be years. If you are in doubt as to whether an investment opportunity is genuine, it is essential to seek professional advice. Furthermore, most of these investments are unregulated, so when they fail, as most of them do, the chances are you will have little or no course of action to seek compensation. Your money will quite literally have disappeared, never to be seen again.

And don't be tempted to take action into your own hands. Even if you can get in front of the 'salesperson' who convinced you to invest, they will know all the tricks in the book and you will soon find the full force of the law bearing down on you, even if you are tempted to threaten them. They know how to wriggle out of every hole they find themselves in and remarkably you will find that they appear to have no resources to pay you back either. They have a habit of not actually retaining any assets in their own name. Funny that, isn't it?

In summary, just avoid these schemes at all cost. They are only ever likely to lead you to high stress levels and the loss of the money you invested. Keep it simple and make sure you understand what you are getting into and how it works.

20 Circle of competence

We are all experts in our own little niches

– Alex Trebek

No one likes to think that they don't know enough about a subject, which can sometimes lead us into doing things that we do not fully understand. Some people go along with a suggestion for fear of other people thinking that they are not very bright. We have all experienced salespeople who attempt to make us feel inadequate if we don't understand something, in an attempt to get us to buy from them.

Avoiding making the mistake of thinking you know enough or allowing a pushy salesperson to persuade you to part with your money is critical to your success on the road to financial freedom. Accepting that you may not know enough and may need to improve on your knowledge or take the advice of a professional expert is essential for success.

How to avoid making a mistake

Firstly, when it comes to planning for financial freedom, it is important to understand that no single person has all of the answers and that includes all of the professional experts out there. Even the professionals are experts in their own niches.

So, recognising that you do not know it all, even though you may have a good understanding in some areas, will stand you in good stead. For example, a residential property investor probably has insufficient knowledge to become a successful property developer. Even though the investment is in the same area, the chances are that they will not have the appropriate skills for the job.

So, what are your natural skills? What are your strengths and what interests you? Some investors like to be hands-on and want to understand exactly how everything works, whilst others are far more passive and prefer a less complicated financial strategy. What type of person are you?

Whatever type of person you are and whatever your preferred investment style, work on continually developing your knowledge in that area. Not only will you become more successful, but you also become far more adept at identifying good opportunities and even better at avoiding the bad ones.

A great example of this is investors in the stock market. In the dull and uninteresting times, the wise investor who knows what he is doing will be quietly investing away, even though they are probably not making any headway. Shuttle forward a few years and the market is rising rapidly and the wise investors will either still be investing regularly or may have stopped investing new money altogether.

On the other side of the coin, the investors that do not have the right level of knowledge are steadfastly ignoring the market when it is flat, stating that 'you can't make money on the stock market'. Shuttle forward a few years when the market is in full flight, and all of a sudden they have forgotten their old mantra and pile into the market at the peak. Guess what, the market falls eventually, and they are terribly disappointed and will tell everyone about how the stock market is a rubbish place to invest.

The moral of the story is to know as much as you possibly can before investing in anything. Understand how it works and what may happen in the future. It is essential to be a competent investor in whatever area you are going to invest. Far too many people invest without having sufficient knowledge and wonder why it does not work out well for them.

In summary, the rule here is to understand what your level of competency is, work on developing it and avoid areas that you have little knowledge of.

21 Recognising you have made a mistake

A person who never made a mistake never tried anything new

– Albert Einstein

A wise man learns from others' mistakes, or so they say. In my experience this is not necessarily quite true. Yes, it is certainly true that we can all learn from others' mistakes, but the real learning points come from making our own mistakes and learning from those. Because they are often quite painful, these are the lessons that really stick and that we learn well from. The emotions that we have when we lose or fail at something are extremely strong and the effects can stay with us for a long time if we are not careful.

We can read all the books available about how to achieve success, we can learn all the theories, but when it comes to the crunch it is our own mistakes and errors of judgement that teach us the most.

When it comes to creating financial freedom for ourselves and our families it is important to accept that we are not always going to make the right decisions. Almost certainly, what we think is the right thing to do today will sooner or later be the wrong thing. The problem that many investors face is that they believe that once they have found a strategy that works for them they just need to keep doing the same thing repeatedly and their wealth will just continue to increase.

Unfortunately, the universe does not work quite like that and what works today will not always work tomorrow. Wealth creation rarely or never works continuously over time. If it did, don't you think that everyone would follow the same path? If it did work like that, very soon that strategy would become much less effective and possibly turn from being very profitable to loss-making. A classic tale of this is investing into a rapidly rising investment market, when everyone and their granny are buying shares. Eventually, it all comes to an end and lots of people lose money. The same can be said for property investing. For the last thirty years property growth has outstripped income growth enormously and many investors are now of the belief that this will continue forever, leading many people to buy more property. Will the growth continue? Only time will tell, but I am fairly convinced that economically this cannot continue, not to mention that government policy is now specifically focused on containing this rapid growth.

So, from a financial freedom perspective and when increasing your wealth it is important to understand that you will make mistakes, you will make errors of judgement. How you deal with the mistakes that you make over time will have a critical effect on how successful you will be.

However, the problem is that people do not like to admit that they have made a mistake and either continue to make more mistakes or do nothing to rectify the problem.

This is the classic dilemma that investors often face: 'If your investment fell in value buy 20%, what would you do next?'

I can tell you from experience over the last thirty years, something like 80% of investors will sit tight and wait for the investment to improve. That may well be the right answer and the right thing to do. However, more answers are required before making that decision. The 80% are making that decision from an emotional perspective rather than a factual one. It is not in most people's makeup to accept losing money and they will do almost anything to avoid it. But it gets worse. Investors in this situation tell themselves that they will hold the investment until it breaks even and then sell, which may take years.

If the investment falls further, the investors' emotions are really put to the test, and depending upon their level of risk tolerance if it falls far enough many people completely lose their nerve and sell their investment at the worst possible time, crystalising a huge loss. All this comes down to emotion and not being prepared to accept that the original decision may have been flawed and incorrect. It is a fundamental human character trait that most of us just don't like to accept that we have made a mistake.

So, how do we avoid making this mistake?

The key to avoiding falling into this trap is to first of all accept that some of the decisions you make will be wrong and some of them will be right. Letting profitable investments continue to run is clearly a good strategy. After all, who would sell something that continues to be successful without good reason?

On the other hand, getting out of a losing investment that no longer makes sense sooner rather than later could save you a lot of money in the long run. Not to mention, the money that is sitting in a losing investment right now could be moved to a winning investment. This is the opportunity cost of not doing anything.

When it comes to a losing investment, it is important to avoid being emotional, accept the fact that it is losing and work on understanding why it is not working and whether it really is the right investment to hold. Take the emotion out of the equation and look at the facts.

For example, let's say you decide to invest in a holiday home set in a beautiful Devonshire seaside town, but after a few seasons the property struggles to rent during the high season and you are now having to add money every month to keep it going. The emotional investors tell themselves that it is only short-term and next year will be better. But, what if lots of other people have had the same idea and have also bought holiday lets and the market is now flooded, driving rents down? Doesn't look quite so good, does it?

The savvy investors will more than likely look at the facts and decide whether it is worth continuing with, or could the money be working better for them invested elsewhere?

In summary, don't become overly attached to your investments; just because they worked before does not mean that they will continue to work in the future. Be sure of your facts when an investment is not working and limit your losses before they become so big that your actions become paralysed.

22 Comfort zones are a sure way to lose the game

No one ever made a difference by being the same as everyone else

– P T Barnham

Starting to invest for the first time can be a very daunting experience and it is very easy to make mistakes, of which there are many kinds. Avoiding the pitfalls at the start of your journey is essential, so understanding what the early simple mistakes are is crucial if you are going to be successful on the journey to financial freedom.

One of the biggest mistakes I see new investors make, is 'playing it too safe'. It is perfectly understandable to be very cautious to start with, but this is more than likely a big mistake.

Let's look at this in little more detail as it will help you understand why being careful and cautious to start with is probably going to be the wrong strategy for you. Let's say you are just starting on your financial journey and that you have around twenty to thirty years to build up your wealth. The new investor, not understanding what pitfalls to avoid, often starts with a very low-risk strategy or probably does not invest as much as they can justifiably afford. Surprisingly, I see many new and young investors saving the majority of their long-term money in cash deposit accounts, which as we all know currently pay very little indeed. In fact, inflation will almost certainly be eroding the purchasing power of that money.

The new investor is very concerned about losing money in the short term rather than considering the options over the medium and long term, but this is a big mistake. Of course, a paper loss may occur in the short term, but if the money is not required for several decades ahead, it does not really matter if in the short term the value goes up and down. Many investors find it too uncomfortable watching the frequent ups and downs in the value. Whilst it may be uncomfortable to watch, these ups and downs are actually going to work in your favour over the long term. Long-term investors benefit from what is called **'pound cost averaging'**.

'Pound cost averaging' is enormously beneficial to investors provided that the value over time increases overall. The short-term ups and downs will mean that in the periods where the value goes down, any money invested during that period will buy more shares than if the value had just gone up in a straight line over time. If the price is rising all the time, fewer shares will be purchased each time money is invested.

Provided that the value is higher at the end of the term than the starting point, you will have acquired a larger number of shares than if you had invested the money in a low-risk investment that has little variation in the price over time.

The power of 'pound cost averaging' and the ups and downs in the value of an investment work powerfully for the investor.

The mistake that many new investors make is that they try to avoid the ups and downs and as a consequence choose low-risk investments. This means that the value of their investment will often be of a lower value at the end of the period that if some amount of risk had been taken.

That is not to say that you should continually take risk. Taking a higher level of risk in the early years can work very well and as your investment wealth gets larger. As you get closer to the time when you will need the money to live on, you should consider reducing your level of risk. As your wealth increases it is important to consider how much risk you are taking and to reduce the risk over time. It may be that once you have achieved your goal of financial freedom, you have removed much of the risk from your investment portfolio altogether.

In summary, taking insufficient risk in the early years is unlikely to serve you well and conversely taking too much risk later on may also permanently damage your wealth, from which you may never be able to recover. Some investors facing a financial dilemma take too much risk too late in their journey in a vain attempt to catch up. This should really be avoided at all costs.

23 The rule of 25

If you don't know where you are going, you might end up somewhere else

– Yogi Berra

If I've been asked this question once, I have been asked it a thousand times or more.

'How much do I need to retire?'

At some time or other most of us have thought about this question or have asked someone else the question. From the man down the pub to a professional adviser, it is THE question that perplexes many people and the answers vary wildly from a few hundred thousand pounds to millions.

As you would expect, the answer is different for everyone and there are a few variables that need to be taken into consideration, ranging from how long you intend to be retired to how much you think you may spend in retirement.

Before trying to work out how much you need to build up to achieve financial freedom and retire, working out what you will spend is critical if you want to work out how much you need.

Working out your current expenditure is a great start to your planning, and a simple spreadsheet will help you get to a reasonably accurate figure of how much you are currently spending. So, start with a list of your current spending. Here is a list to get you started; however, you may have additional items you wish to add to the list. All the items should be the monthly cost and if the expenditure is annual divide the figure by 12.

Mortgage or rent payment
Gas and electricity
Water
Telephone and broadband
TV licence
Mobile phone
Council tax

Grocery costs
Eating out costs
Clothes
Hairdressing

Christmas spending
Birthday spending
Holiday costs
Books
Gym membership
Sports equipment and events
Entertainment

Car finance
Car insurance
House insurance
Life insurance
Pension contribution
Investment saving

Clearly the list is not exhaustive and there are likely to be more items you need to add, but it is a very good place to start.

Once you have added up the monthly amount, you need to remove any items that you will not have to pay for once you are retired.

This will give you an indication of how much you may be spending once you are retired. Taking this figure, multiply it by 12 to give you an annual expenditure amount.

For example, if your total spending now amounts to £3,500 a month and the amount of expenditure after the removal of pre-retirement spending amounts to £1,000, the post-retirement amount will be £2,500 a month. Taking the £2,500 a month and multiplying this by 12 will give you a minimum spending need of £30,000 a year. So, if you were to retire today, this is the amount of income you would need so that you could retire and no longer have to work.

It may sound like a very challenging amount of income to replace from your investments; however, there is another factor that you need to take into consideration.

If you are eligible for a full state pension, this amount can be offset against the £30,000 requirement in the example above. The situation may also be improved if both you and your partner will both qualify for a state pension. Let's say that the full state pension amounts to £8,500 a year each.

If you are likely to receive two state pensions, the revised income need will be £13,000 from your investments. This is £30,000 less £8,500 twice.

So now that we know how much income is required in addition to the two state pensions, we now need to calculate how much capital is needed to provide the £13,000 a year of income.

The very simple rule of thumb is to multiply the £13,000 by 25.

£13,000 x 25 = £325,000

This is the amount of money that needs to be available for you to start to draw on once you retire. There is, however, one major caveat. This calculation only works provided that your retirement coincides with the time that your state pension begins. If it is your intention to retire before the state pension starts, the amount of money you need will need to be in excess of the £325,000 calculated in the above example.

To calculate the amount needed in this situation is a much more complex calculation which we do not have time to go into right now. However, I am sure that you get the picture of the amount that you need to build up.

In summary, calculating how much you need can be quite simple, even if creating it is more challenging. Take your anticipated spending in retirement, less what you expect from the state pension and multiply the amount by 25. This will give you the minimum target amount that you need to be aiming for to achieve financial freedom.

24 The 4% rule

*An idea in your head is just a dream; a goal
written down is a plan of action*

— Martin Dodd

In the previous section, we worked out how much of a capital base we need to aim for in order to achieve financial freedom and be able to retire. However, this raises another question, and I get asked this question quite frequently as well. It is a justifiably important question because if you get this wrong you could either run out of money before you die or have far too much money left when you die. Neither of these scenarios are what any of us really want to happen.

The question that I get asked is this.

'How do I make sure that I do not run out of money in retirement?'

When people do not know the answer to this question, more often than not people live far to frugally and do not live life to the full. Perhaps unsurprisingly, many people who have saved diligently for their retirement do not enjoy their retirement fully as they worry about running out of money during their lifetime. If that was you, now wouldn't that be a little sad? Imagine all of the things that you could have enjoyed or perhaps done with your family.

There are three types of people I encounter in retirement:

1. Those that don't have enough and run out of money;

2. Those that have too much and end up with far too much left at the end of their lives;

3. And those that get it just right, enjoying their retirement years to the full.

If we can find the answer to the question of avoiding running out of money and not being too frugal, hopefully you can be one of those people in the third category – the ones I call 'getting it just right'.

So, imagine that you have built up your retirement fund using the rule of 25. And let's say you need an investment portfolio of £325,000, as in the example in the previous section. To give yourself the best possibility of not running out of money, you should withdraw no more than 4% of the investment portfolio each year.

There are two reasons why this is important. Firstly, by the time you have achieved financial freedom and are in retirement, you should start to, or will have already, moved your investments to a much lower level of investment risk. Once you are in retirement, there will be little opportunity to replace any lost capital should your investment portfolio suffer a significant loss of value.

Secondly, even if you achieved no investment returns during your retirement years, withdrawing 4% or less a year would mean that your capital would last for a full twenty-five years before being fully exhausted. For most people that would probably last most, if not all, of their retirement years.

If, however, you want to achieve financial freedom and to retire at a much younger age, not only will you need a much larger capital amount to provide you with an income, but you should also consider a lower level of withdrawal than 4% a year.

In summary, a controlled withdrawal of income from your investment portfolio is essential to avoid running out of money or have too much left at the end of your life. By checking your investment values and the amount of income you need each year you will also help ensure that you are one of those people that 'get it just right'.

25 Practising your dreams before trying them for real

Look before you leap

– John Heywood

A new phenomenon has started to happen in the world of financial freedom and retiring to live the life of your choice. You may have come across it and not realised, but I can assure you that it is very real and is happening far more often than you probably realise.

Have you noticed how there are more and more people that are often working casual jobs that are over the normal retirement age and in some cases way over retirement age?

Some of these people may never have retired as they quite literally are unable to afford to. However, there is a growing group of people that have retired once and have now returned to work. Many of these people are doing it not because they need the mental stimulation, but because economically they have little choice. In other words, they have miscalculated how much money they need in retirement and have little choice other than to return to the workforce.

This phenomenon is now being referred to as 'un-retiring'.

This group of people have no choice other than to start work again just to cover their cost of living. Sadly, once retired, the options available are often reduced and skillsets advance and technology starts to take over in the work-place, leading to the un-retirees having to take on casual work.

So, what is the answer to avoiding this potentially happening to you?

The reality for most people is that they just let retirement happen to them. They perhaps did little forward planning and retired when they were either told to or when conventional wisdom suggested that they did. They quite literally did not plan what life would be like once that regular monthly pay cheque came to an end a new chapter of their lives began.

There was no smooth path, there was perhaps no planned glide path into retirement and as a consequence it sometimes goes horribly wrong finan-cially, not to mention the impact it can have on personal relationships.

If retirement was like most other things in life, we would practise it before we did it for real. If it was a marathon we were about to embark on, there is little chance that you would not have done any practising before race day. Almost every would-be marathon runner would have practised and trained for the day.

Unfortunately, very few people practise their retirement before they get to THE DAY. Now, wouldn't that be a good idea – practise your retirement before you actually retire. By practising your retirement before you stopped working or running your business would be an excellent way of testing whether it was all going to work out or not. Rather like a marathon runner doing a few long runs close to the distance before race day, at the very least the marathon runner will have an idea of what race day may be like.

I recommend practising for retirement for six months before you actually retire.

Based on the calculations that we made in the previous sections, you should have a reasonable idea of how much money you will be spending once you have retired. As you get ready to retire, and most certainly before it actually happens, take six months practising living on how much you expect to have coming in once you are retired. It really is the acid test before taking the plunge for real. It is far better to find out before the event that you can or cannot live on the income that you will have coming in.

Rather like the would-be marathon runner, if you run out of energy and have to stop at the fifteen-mile mark, you probably know in advance that the marathon will be too much for you and some more preparation needs to happen before the day.

In summary, practise living on the amount of income you expect to spend in retirement. If it is insufficient, you know that you have to either revise how much you are going to be spending or you need to have a larger pot of money to draw from once you retire.

26 The wealth equation: wealth = resources + technology

Money isn't the most important thing in the world, but it's right up there with oxygen

— Zig Ziglar

It is probably more important than it has ever been, to start planning to become financially free as soon as possible. All too often I hear people saying that there is no need to start planning for the future just yet as they have plenty of time to worry about things like that. This opinion could not be further from the truth.

Whilst there are probably more opportunities than there have been in the past, there are far more demands on our resources than ever before as well. In addition to that, whilst opportunity exists it is harder to achieve financial freedom unless you start early and have a system to continually grow your wealth.

I often hear people say that 'money is not important' or 'money won't buy you happiness'.

Whilst I agree with the second statement, the first statement could not be further from the truth and the lack of money probably results in more stress and relationship problems in society today.

With this in mind, we can benefit enormously from using all sorts of resources to help us increase our wealth on the road to financial freedom.

Even using simple spreadsheets to track the development and growth of our wealth is very powerful, not only so that we can see how far we have got, but it also helps us keep motivated and enthusiastic. We should use the technology available to help us track our wealth creation and to keep the process automated as far as possible.

Starting with an asset statement

Many people think that asset statements are something that businesses and wealthy people do. However, this is something that we should all do, as seeing what we have written down is far more motivational and effective than simply holding this information in our heads.

An asset statement should include all our assets, all of our liabilities and show the net amount. Using a spreadsheet to do this is extremely effective and can be kept continuously up to date. The table below is a very simple example of an asset statement to get you started.

Asset Statement	Asset	Liability
House	£350,000.00	£100,000.00
Contents	£20,000.00	
Savings	£30,000.00	
Investments	£100,000.00	
Pensions	£200,000.00	
Total	£700,000.00	£100,000.00
Net Assets	£600,000.00	

As your wealth begins to accumulate, your asset statement will become more complicated, which gives you an even bigger reason to maintain the statement. We have all heard of fabulously successful people running out of money. In most cases this is not because they do not earn enough money but because they do not fully understand what their assets are, where they are and what they are doing for them.

Once you have created your asset statement, maintaining an accurate spreadsheet detailing your regular expenditure is also very important. The expenditure spreadsheet is important for two reasons. Firstly, it will help you clearly understand what you are spending and on what, and secondly – and this is possibly even more important – it will help you identify 'leakage'.

'Leakage' is the amount of money that just disappears every month and does not appear as any of your regular expenditure. This happens to just about all of us and can be very useful in helping us identify how much we waste every month. This could be additional resources that you could be putting towards your financial freedom plan.

The table below is a very simple example of an expenditure spreadsheet to get you started.

Expenditure	
Mortgage	£1,000
Council tax	£200
Gas	£75
Electricity	£50
Water	£30
TV & broadband	£60
Food	£600
Eating out	£150
Birthday gifts	£50
Christmas gifts	£50
Gym membership	£30
Hair	£100
Holidays	£200
Pension investment	£350
Monthly savings	£150
Total	£3,095

This is quite a simple table and there are probably other items which you can add so that you have a more accurate idea of where your money is being spent.

In summary, to achieve financial freedom you first need to know where you are right now and what resources you have to help build on your wealth. A personal asset statement will help you understand where you are now, and the expenditure spreadsheet will help you understand what you are spending and help identify what extra resources you could be adding to your wealth.

A sample asset statement and sample expenditure template can be found in Appendices 3 and 4.

27 The power of 3

Everyone can, but not everyone will

– Martin Dodd

Can't afford to or can't afford not to?

Achieving financial freedom, for most people, is not the easiest task in the world and for many it can take time and perseverance. Unfortunately, not everyone has the patience to keep working on their future plans, and many people give up.

I find it quite fascinating that people from similar backgrounds and levels of intelligence often end up in completely different places when it comes to planning for the future. Why is it that given the same start in life, people end up in very different places, from having very little and needing state support, to others who achieve financial freedom beyond their wildest dreams.

In my opinion, there are only a few small things that can make a difference to your future results. The main two are having the ability to keep persevering, and having a plan and sticking to it.

The problem with perseverance at the beginning of the journey is that you often see small results to start with and it is only much further down the line that you start to see big results.

For example, if you have £1,000 invested and you achieve 10% growth in a year, your wealth has only grown by £100. Not exactly very exciting to start with, I am sure you would agree. On the other hand, if you had £100,000 invested and it grew by 10%, your wealth will have increased by £10,000. Far more exciting, wouldn't you agree?

So, how do you keep motivated and remain committed to achieving financial freedom?

It is essential in the early years as you start to build up your wealth to have rules for how your money is invested and stick to them through thick and thin. You must guard against becoming derailed and stay with the program. Just like the marathon runner, a bad training session doesn't mean you should give up. It means you must keep persevering.

If you didn't know where you are going to get to, it would be easy just to give up. However, if you had a program that had a fixed set of rules then you are far more likely to stick to it than if there were no rules to follow.

Here are the rules to follow that are important to keep you on track.

1. Save every month without fail.

2. Know exactly how much you are spending each month.

3. Invest/save a fixed percentage of your income each month.

4. Automate the process to take away the decision-making process.

Unfortunately, many people break just a few, or even all, of these rules, which is why many people never quite achieve financial freedom. They don't save every month and they often don't know how much money they spend every month. If they do save, the amounts are variable, and many do not automate the process. These are all problems, and the last one is a particularly major problem, as without automation the actual act of saving or investing just does not happen at all. And even when it does, it is often too late, and the amounts that need to be invested are just too much. So, they give up. **Automation is the key to success.**

For some, getting their head around automated saving is just too much for them and they prefer to accumulate cash before committing to investing, as they might just need it. Investing for the future should be seen as a necessity, rather than a luxury.

By setting up automated investing, and at a fixed percentage of your income, is an excellent way to build your wealth. However, many people are resistant to this on the basis that they simply cannot afford to save 10% or 15% of their income every month.

Whilst doing this may be very difficult to start with, if you commit to doing this for just three to six months, you will be surprised how quickly you get used to having a reduced amount to spend. The new reduced amount of 85% to 90% of your income will quickly become the norm for you. Most people can quickly get used to less income if they have to. The problem is that most people do not try to do this and don't realise that it is possible to do.

In summary, use the rules of investing to your advantage, let go of the excuses and automate your wealth-building program to become financially free. Have an effective system in place that removes the emotional decisions around how to make sure your money is continuously working for you.

28 Timing is everything – really?

Be greedy when others are fearful. And be fearful when others are greedy

— Warren Buffett

'I'm not going to invest right now because it's not a good time.' I've heard that many times before.

This is the philosophy of the investor who is trying to 'time the market'. This is trying to work out when to get in and when to get out. Quite simply, this is the most dangerous strategy, and one that is almost certainly not going to work over the long term. Of course, some investors have managed to time the market, but this is usually more luck than expert judgement.

Be very wary of so-called 'experts' who tell you that they can time the market. If they could do this, why on earth would they be telling you or anyone else, for that matter? They surely would be keeping the secret for themselves, so that they can increase their wealth and make even more money for themselves.

The expert market timer is more than likely to be a fraud and your money will soon have disappeared altogether. The market timer is most likely to be the person who is looking to get rich quick or sell you the idea that you can get rich quick too. As nice as that may sound, very few people ever achieve getting rich quick.

If you can't time the market, what is the best way to invest?

Avoiding the dangers of 'timing the market' means that you must have a system of investing. Because investing for many people can be, or become, an emotional roller coaster, so systemising how you invest will help you avoid these issues.

I put enormous value on investing on an automated basis every month. This helps you avoid having to make decisions on when is the right time to invest. In some months, the market will be down and in some months the markets will be up. On average, however, over the longer-term markets continue to rise in value. So, do the monthly ups and downs really make that much difference? Over the long term, they will in the end be of little consequence.

Many investors continue to worry about the ups and downs in the short term and all sorts of poor decisions are often made. Investors sometimes panic when the market falls and so they sell out. On the other hand, when the market is rising rapidly, they invest into the market when it is often too late in the day, buying close to or right at the peak. And we all know what happens when a market hits a high point rapidly. Yes, a substantial fall is usually just around the corner. Guess what the inexperienced investor then does? Yes, they sell quickly and usually at a loss and tell everyone that markets don't work and that it is impossible to make money.

I couldn't disagree more.

The successful investor buys continuously through the market's ups and downs and takes little notice of short-term volatility. Short-term market moves are just 'market noise'. Short-term changes in value do not represent any fundamental change in the success or profitability of the companies you have invested in.

The second rule that you need to understand and apply is knowing how much risk you are prepared to accept. Buying individual shares on a tip or timing the market does not really take into account your capacity for risk or your ability to withstand a loss. Knowing how much risk you can live with will guide you towards certain types of investments.

In very simple terms, lower-risk investments include cash and fixed-interest securities and shares are usually of a higher risk. Even within shares, there are lower-risk and high-risk investment options. For example, a FTSE100-listed share is likely to be less risky that a share listed on the Smaller Companies Exchange. Understanding your individual risk is therefore essential.

In summary, avoid trying to time the market at all costs, and automate investing on a regular basis. Also, it is important to understand how much risk you can live with over your time period. As you get closer to your financial freedom date or retirement, you should consider reducing the amount of risk that you take.

29 The three pillars of wealth creation

It always seems impossible until it's done
– Nelson Mandela

The words of Nelson Mandela could not be more true when it comes to achieving financial freedom. For many it always seems such an impossible task, so they either start and fail or never get started at all.

'Live life for today.'

'Money isn't everything.'

'Money doesn't buy you happiness.'

All of the above statements are true, but rather like a complete obsession with money, the quotes above are similarly extreme. A sensible route down the middle is the right path that we should be taking. Working towards our own version of financial freedom is the path we should all be following.

As you have probably gathered by now, financial freedom is best achieved through a systemised and planned approach. Financial freedom is unlikely to happen just by accident, unless you are very lucky.

Financial freedom is not just about creating one big pot of money or investments from which you can live off. Financial freedom is about creating wealth that can be used, or that is needed, for different purposes.

Why do I need money for different purposes?

Building an individual financial freedom plan that is just for you and your family should include three types of money for three different purposes. This also allows you to manage the risk that you are taking with your money.

The different types of money to consider are as follows:

1. Short-term money

2. Medium to long-term money

3. Long-term money

We all need short-term money for a number of reasons. Short-term money is very easily accessible money that is not invested in an asset that exposes you to any risk. Typically, this money should cover your known expenditure for anything from three to twelve months. If something goes drastically wrong in your life, the last thing you want to be worrying about is how to pay for the costs that you had not anticipated.

Additionally, having accessible savings available provides further comfort in knowing that you can easily raise money for any type of expenditure that may come up unexpectedly. This could be to pay for something that you did not expect or to help other family members in a less fortunate position than you. Being financially secure allows you to help others that do not have the savings that you have.

Typically, your short-term money should be held in a deposit account even though you are unlikely to earn all that much interest on the amount held.

Medium- to long-term money/investments fits into that middle ground between short-term savings and long-term investments. Long-term investments are often inaccessible until you reach a certain age and as such are not a lot of use to you in the medium term.

Medium- to long-term investments – and what I mean by this is money that you would ideally not expect to need within the next five years – can be invested in a more speculative way. The object of investing this money is to earn more than inflation and what you could earn by leaving it on deposit. Remember, when you invest money in a deposit-based account there is never going to be any certainty of making much profit, only the potential to earn interest.

Although you may have no specific purpose for this money, you need to be able to access it should the need arise. You may be wondering what you may need the money for in the medium to long term; however, there are always opportunities arising over time that may tempt you to spend your money. The money is invested to work for you, knowing that one day you may wish to withdraw some or all of the capital for another reason.

For example, you may wish to buy a holiday home, a motor home or even a boat! If the money you could have saved has already been spent or has been sat in a deposit account for years, it may be a great deal harder to take advantage of an opportunity in life that arises.

Long-term money is what you are going to use once you have achieved financial freedom, and it is going to form a big part of the income you need in the future. Long-term could be anything from ten years to thirty years or more, so you can afford to be more speculative with this money for a substantial part of this period. This type of investing should almost certainly be set up on an automated basis, so that you can avoid having to make any decisions month by month. That is not to say that you should ignore what it is doing and how it is performing. Only the investing of the money should be automated.

If at the end of year, you still have spare resources that could be invested, this can still be invested in either your medium- or long-term pots. Always make sure that your short-term deposit money is kept topped up, which you can do from either income or moving some of your medium-term money to your deposit savings.

In summary, save and invest your money for three separate purposes. It will make you far more financially robust and give you flexibility with how to manage your money. I come across many people who have far too much invested for the short term and are also investing for the long term. Fewer people have medium-term money available, which could mean that they are missing out on some of life's opportunities.

30 Avoiding fool's gold and killer strategies

A fool and his money are soon parted

– proverb

Wouldn't it be great if we could achieve financial freedom quickly, painlessly, easily **and** without taking any risks, by just following a specific plan? Wouldn't life just be fantastic? We could really live the life, do all those fantastic things that everyone dreams about.

I am sorry to break it to you, but for 99.9% of people 'getting rich quick' is just not going to happen. 'Getting rich' – or as I prefer to call it becoming financially free – for most of us takes time, takes effort, and certainly requires having a plan and sticking to it.

However, that does not stop a whole army of people out there who will tell you that if you follow 'their' plan, you too can become super rich very quickly. And even better, they will tell you that they can do it without any great effort and it will happen in a very short period of time, just so long as you follow their specific program. And of course, to get access to all their secrets, you will have to part with some of your hard-earned money, and it won't be cheap.

The first thing to consider is this. Why would a so-called 'overnight' success want to let anyone in on the way to get-rich-quick? Surely if they really knew how to do it, they certainly wouldn't be telling anyone else how it is done. If they share their secrets, they risk diluting their formula, which would affect their continued riches. If they really knew the answer, they would be sitting on their superyacht in some blue ocean resort, living the life of luxury. They absolutely would not be telling anyone else how to do it or selling you their ideas.

If it looks too good to be true, it probably is. I would go as far as saying that if it looks too good to be true, it isn't true.

When it comes to getting great results in anything in this life, there is no substitute for hard effort and time. Nothing looks more like an overnight success than someone that works hard for a sustained period and sticks doggedly to their plan.

That's not to say that if a great opportunity arises you shouldn't take advantage of it. Many people have missed opportunities in the past because they are unsure or are suspicious of an opportunity.

So, how do you spot a scam and how do you identify a great opportunity?

Firstly, it is important to recognise that we can all become potential victims of a scam, but we can do much to minimise the chances of becoming an unwitting victim. Knowing what to look out for will certainly reduce the chances of getting caught out.

Here is what you should look out for.

1. Investment opportunities or 'get-rich' programs that are on limited-time offer only: This type of offering will try to get you to part with your money quickly, by using scarcity. 'If you don't act now, you will miss the chance.' This type of offer is trying to discourage you from making a full and fair assessment of what the offer is.

2. Investment opportunities offered over the phone from someone you have never heard of before: Boiler-room investment offerings still exist, and they use high-pressure sales techniques to try and convince you to invest. They will nearly always tell you, 'You need to do it now before it's too late.' Watch the film The Wolf of Wall Street if you are not sure how high-pressure sales techniques are used by the unscrupulous.

3. The investment returns promised seem too high: The promoters of get-rich-quick schemes know that people are tempted by and attracted to high investment returns, so they play on these emotions. So, if the returns seem extraordinary, chances are that what they are trying to sell you is either unrealistic at best, or more likely a fraud.

4. The investment offers a guaranteed investment return: All investments carry some level of investment risk, so if you are offered an investment that has a guaranteed investment return, you need to know how that guarantee is backed up. The reality is that investments go up and down in value on a day-to-day basis, so any guaranteed return should be viewed with some scepticism, unless you know clearly how that guarantee will work.

5. Investments that promise to beat the market: Any investment, whether it be stocks and shares or property, that promises to beat the market is more than likely to be some form of scam or at the very least not telling you the truth. Beating the market all of the time is impossible as it would require investment decisions to be correct virtually all of the time. As I have said before, it is impossible to time the market, and anyone that tells you that they can should be avoided if you want to not only keep your money but also avoid major disappointment.

In summary, we are all motivated to some extent to have more, and it would be easy to get drawn into making a financial decision based on an idea that you could shortcut the process by following a special formula. Over the decades many people have lost huge amounts of money because they have been offered the chance to beat the odds. When it comes to scams, always remember that those that are promoting them and selling them are professional sellers and you are an amateur buyer.

There have been numerous frauds over the years, from Nigerian money scams to envelope-stuffing scams, most of which we are aware of and avoid. However, there are new scams appearing all of the time, so being vigilant is more important than ever. I have said it already, but if it looks too good to be true, it probably is. Keep that in mind and you increase your chances of avoiding being caught out by a scammer.

31 Having a big enough reason to succeed

The secret to success is enthusiasm

— Walter Chrysler

Sadly, financial freedom eludes many, if not most, people as they do not have a big enough reason to succeed and are easily distracted from the job in hand. Just wanting to have money and to be financially free is probably not going to be enough to motivate you to focus fully on the end goal. After all, money saved for the future is only deferred spending, and we all know that spending today is much more fun than thinking about what you could be spending it on in twenty years' time.

The problem that affects many people is maintaining enthusiasm for the future and their financial security for what will be, for many of us, a long time – that could be for three or four decades. How do we keep motivated about a plan for so long?

My belief is that in order to keep up the enthusiasm for such a long time, a balanced approach is necessary. Without some rewards on the way, most of us will waver off the path to success and some of us will never get back on that path. I don't want you to be one of those people, so we need some strategies to keep us motivated.

When your motivation wavers, it is good to go back to the reasons why you started down the road of creating financial freedom for yourself in the first place. At the highest level, there are two motivating factors that drive all of us. We are either driven away from something, i.e. pain, or we are driven towards something, i.e. gain. Understanding whether you are motivated more by the pain or the gain is important to help you succeed. Which one are you?

Beyond pain or gain, we need some more tools in the box to keep us on track, and I have set out below some of the things that you should be thinking about.

1. Your plan for financial freedom must be your plan. It must be what you want, not somebody else's plan. It's rather like taking a job because your family think you should, or because it 'kind of' makes sense to you. You know that you will probably not be satisfied with the outcome. Your financial plan must be about what you really want and taking your time to actually decide what it is will help you achieve your goals.

2. Be careful who you discuss your future plans with as there are always going to be doubters that can lead you away from the path. Some people call this 'lobster pot' syndrome. As the lobster tries to escape the pot, the others try to pull it back. It is really important that you do not allow anyone to pull you back. Remember those famous words we've all heard: 'You can't do that.' We all need to be careful who we share our goals with and be sure that they will give us their support, even if it is just verbal encouragement. At the beginning of your journey to financial freedom, the last thing we need is people unintentionally or intentionally diverting us away from our plans.

   Unfortunately, it's just human nature to be less than enthusiastic about another person's dreams and I am certain that most of the time it is not intentional. Nevertheless, only confide in your believers and positive people as they will want you to succeed.

3. I am a big believer in rewarding achievements during the journey. If the ultimate destination is ten, twenty or thirty years from now, that's a long time and it would be very easy to become lost or disillusioned along the way. To help improve our chances of success, I recommend that you reward yourself at milestones to celebrate how far you have come. The celebration does not need to be extravagant or expensive, it just needs to be something you don't do on a regular basis. Rewards, as we all know, work as a great incentive to keep doing something, especially if the ultimate goal is a long way into the future.

I'll let you decide what your rewards could be. Just don't spend too much as that will set your plans back.

4. Sometimes when we are planning for a great future, it's easy to forget where we have come from. The reason why we think like this is that it's very easy to just focus on where we are heading. It is therefore a good idea to take a step back from time to time and look back to where we started from and see how far we have come. Sometimes we need to look back to see what our achievements have really been. After a reflection on your journey so far, it's time to get back to the plan and building for the future.

5. Never try and keep up with the Joneses. From time to time we have all been guilty of looking at what other people are doing, or shall I say what they are outwardly projecting, and none more so in the holiday season when everyone is posting idyllic pictures of sun-drenched beaches and fantastic holidays. It would be easy to become envious, especially if you have already been on your holiday! The temptation may be to try and keep up, but you have a plan that you need to stick to. For all you know, they may have no plan and are living 100% for today. I have over the years met hundreds of people who completely live their lives for today and I am not saying they

are wrong; it's just not for me. And I guess it's not for you either, as you are reading this book.

6. At the end of our lives, most of us would like to be remembered for something and for some of us that means leaving a legacy, either to our families or to charity. The legacy we leave behind can be a big motivation. Whilst we should be focused on our own goals, remembering that we want to leave a legacy is a powerful motivation that is sometimes forgotten. Keeping that in our minds will help keep us striving to achieve the financial goals we have set for ourselves.

In summary, building wealth, becoming rich, whatever you want to call it, just for money's sake may not be enough to keep you motivated. We all know people that are just motivated by money; however, in my view this is not enough to succeed. We all need the 'extra' ingredient to keep us fully focused on the job in hand. Your motivations are probably different from mine as they are from the next person. Your job is to find that trigger to keep you motivated and enthusiastic and you will dramatically improve your chances of success.

32 What to do should things go wrong

Always carry an umbrella

– unknown

It's a fact of life: Not everything goes to plan and sometimes things go wrong. The question is …

'How will you deal with something when it starts going wrong, and will you still be able to stick to the plan?'

In addition to things going wrong, it's also important to remember that we are only human, and we make mistakes; we all make errors of judgement.

Accepting both that things just go wrong and sometimes that we make mistakes will help us keep on track to financial freedom.

Sadly, at the first sign of trouble far too many people just give up, saying things like, **'It's just too hard'** or **'I don't need to do this'** or **'It's pointless doing this, as I may not be here in the future anyway'**. Giving up on our dreams and plans for the future could be all too easy if it gets difficult and plenty do give up. The road to success can be very lonely as many people do give up on the way.

It is a simple question that we all have to ask ourselves. Are we in it to succeed and work through all the hurdles on the way, or are we going to let the challenging times divert us from the journey?

My guess is that if you have got this far, you are going to be determined, so we need to know what to do and how to react when things are not going in the right direction.

But let's first of all understand the reasons why things go wrong, and there are only two reasons when it comes to the management and creation of wealth:

1. The economic climate means that everyone is suffering.

2. You or your investment advisers have made the wrong decision.

As you can see, the two are very different and as such require a different response.

The first scenario is going to affect everyone that invests at some point in time during their financial journey and if you are investing for the long term this could happen quite a few times. As we know this is almost inevitably going to happen, we all have to accept that we cannot avoid these occasions. Quite often they do not last all that long and investments often recover far more quickly than people expect.

Often when investment values fall, people move from being optimistic one day to overly pessimistic the next. Did the world really change that much since you went to sleep the night before? Probably not. So, if the reasons to invest have not fundamentally changed and the global economy has not changed overnight then there is little reason to be overly concerned. Sitting tight is the name of the game, and remembering that you are invested for the long term.

What you should always consider, though, is how much risk can you tolerate from an emotional perspective. How much risk I can live with could be very different from what you can live with. Even though it makes sense to sit tight, not all of us can do this and can become extremely uncomfortable if the value of our investments fall significantly. So, when we are investing, we need to know what level of risk or fall in the value would keep us awake at night.

For some of us, any fall would cause us concern. Understanding our limits is very important, so if a 5%, a 10%, or a fall of more than 20% would concern you, how much risk you take with your investment is critical. Otherwise if something goes wrong, the chances are that you will want to sell your investments and get out. And the only home then for your money will be in a deposit account, which we all know earns very little and will probably be losing value after inflation is taken into account.

It is really important to position our investments so that we can avoid the emotional rollercoaster that changes in the value of your investment may cause you. Or at least minimise the chance of it happening as far as possible.

The second problem is dealing with a mistake or error of judgement that has been made. It is a different problem and needs to be considered in a different way. Firstly, it is essential to admit that no one can get every decision correct – we are all going to make mistakes.

A technique that I use is to keep my investments under review continuously. I don't check them daily, but I do check them every month usually on the first of the month. I want to know how each investment has performed and how it is performing compared to its peer group. If something is not right, I want to know more, such as why it is not performing and what the likely outcome will be. If an investment continues to underperform, eventually it will have to be disposed of even if that means I have to take a loss.

Many investors hold onto losing investments because they cannot accept making a loss. The rational goes something like this: 'I will keep the investment until it gets back to the amount I invested.' Sound familiar?

There are two problems with doing this. Firstly, it could be a very long time before the value increases, and if it was a poor investment in the first place then how much money could have been made with a better performing investment? Holding onto a losing or non-performing investment could prove very costly.

The second problem is that things could get a whole lot worse. Imagine if you had an investment that had fallen by 10% and it fell by a further 15%. If your tolerance to loss was set at 10% and it was now at a loss of 25%, how would you feel? Pretty awful, I'd imagine.

Do you know how much an investment must increase by to recover a loss of 25%? Some people think that it needs to back up by 25% to recover the loss. The investment actually has to increase by 33.3% to get back to the original value from the low point. That could take years and years, so sitting on a bad investment is never going to be a good idea. Sometimes we just have to accept that we have made a poor decision, move on and get out. The opportunities elsewhere may be much better.

The investment that has fallen by 25% may get even worse and often the investor who was holding on for a recovery to the break-even point may completely lose their nerve and finally sell with an even bigger loss of more than 25%. This type of investor often never returns to the market and will hold all their money in cash for evermore.

To protect yourself from losses, it is important to hold some of your money on deposit. This is your short-term protection money and helps you keep your nerve if the markets move against you. This is your umbrella for a rainy day. As sure as it is going to rain one day, the value of your investments will also fall in value at some point, even for the savviest of investors.

Always keep a reasonably healthy reserve on deposit to calm the nerves, and it will also be very useful if a buying opportunity arises that you can take advantage of.

In summary, we all need to accept that losses will occur, and we need to be mentally ready for them. We also need to know the reasons why the loss has happened and have a plan to deal with them. Be ready to get out for the right reasons and always hold some cash reserves.

33 Luck? Choices? Ripples? Forks?

Fortune favours the bold

— Latin proverb

Contentment is the killer of ambition and no more so than when it comes to FINANCIAL FREEDOM. But why is that? Most of us are happy being just who we are, without striving to push ourselves further.

On the flip side of that is 'Necessity is the mother of invention'. But how do we make FINANCIAL FREEDOM a MUST? How do we build it into our everyday lives?

I have studied the reluctance to financially plan for years and would go as far as saying that around 80% of us just can't face the issue or cannot switch our minds onto what they need to do. A huge part of that is probably caused by fear of the unknown – fear that if we try to become financially secure we might just fail. So, many of us just don't really take the subject seriously enough and allow our lives just to happen to us.

Many of us are afraid to admit that we have an underlying belief that many successful people are successful simply because 'they were born into money' or 'had a great start in life'. Very often this is far from the truth as many financially secure people have created it through their own efforts; they have built it with their own bare hands.

The truth is, success isn't something that we are born with; certainly not for most of us.

Success and financial freedom is something that most of us can achieve with the right combination of hard work, dedication and a plan to succeed.

Looking further beyond hard work and dedication, there are four other life-changing ways you can start on your road to financial freedom today. There are four critical mindsets you must have firmly implanted in your psyche to get the results you are looking for.

Understand these four success factors and within no time at all you will be much better equipped to succeed on your financial freedom journey.

1. There is no such thing as luck

Being lucky is not a real thing really. It is an excuse that some people make for other people being successful. We don't want to think like that. Unfortunately, too many of us are fascinated by the concept of luck. If we believe in luck, we will not be fully focused on keeping to our plan and the chances are we will not succeed. Believing in luck is like playing the lottery week after week in the hope that your numbers will come up for you.

Let go of believing that luck will come your way and keep focused on your financial plan; remain focused on the end goal.

It is really important to intimately understand exactly where you are headed, or financial freedom will evade you.

Achieving financial freedom is one of the few things in life people leave to luck. Just about everything else we do in life we plan for. No one leaves their holiday plans to chance or luck, so it is essential that financial freedom is not left to luck either.

So, if you were not born with a silver spoon in your mouth, don't leave your future to the chance of getting lucky.

2. There are only choices to be made

To become financially free is to constantly face choices. At the very highest level, the choices are to spend it or to invest it. Too much spending and the chances are that you will start to hope you get lucky, and we don't want that, do we?

The cold, hard truth is that we need to be serious about our choices, meaning we have to commit to achieving financial freedom. If you have a dream, be committed. You can't go at it half-heartedly and expect to achieve financial freedom. It's impossible to just go for partial financial freedom. You have to be serious, even though you will need to live a balanced life for today and also the future. There are millions of other people who have the same dreams as you but, are they able to make the right choices between living for now or the future?

This means being committed completely towards your goal of financial freedom. Striving for what you want for tomorrow rather than what you would like today. This is your CHOICE.

Everyone faces obstacles, and many will give up and stop making the right choices. Our job is to find a way to overcome the obstacles and to make the right choices.

3. The power of ripples

We all massively underestimate the power of ripples. We've all thrown a stone into a pond and watched how the ripples start as a very small circle and spread outwards. The original ripples move off into the distance, but the effect of the ripples goes on and on.

Financial freedom starts with a ripple effect. It may start small and may not look like much, but with time, perseverance and sticking to the plan, success comes in the end. At the beginning when you have invested your £1,000 and it grows by 10%, you've made £100, which is probably not that exciting. But when you have reached £100,000 or £200,000, 10% growth starts to become an exciting number. These are the ripples we need to be patient for and not give up on too soon. Financial freedom can be a long and winding road, with twists and turns, bumps and walls, and every obstacle you could imagine. Just remember the ripples – they are your friend.

Believe me, there are going to be many obstacles along your road to success. You will stumble from time to time and people will tell you your plans are no good, but what do they know? You have a plan.

Every person who has achieved financial freedom in this world has gone through this, and when faced with problems they have all told themselves, 'I'm going to keep going. Failure is not an option.'

4. We all face forks in the road

Which way do we go? This way or that? It's just like driving a car on a journey without a map. Just like going on a road trip, there are many ways to get to your destination. Financial freedom is just like a road trip: there are going to be many forks in the road.

We are all going to have to make decisions on whether we should turn left or right.

Making the decision on which way to turn is going to be different for all of us, but what I can say is this: We have to take some turns and sometimes they will be the right one and sometimes they will be the wrong one. But choices there will be, and through our journey to financial freedom we are going to have to keep making them. And just because the road looks to be the right one, it doesn't mean it is always going to be the correct way. Sometimes we are going to take another fork off in another direction. That is just a fact of life.

Many people are happy with 'just enough', but will you really be happy with 'just enough'?

The best experiences we all have in life are never 'just enough'. The best things in life are really special and are definitely worth striving for.

Those that have already journeyed the road to financial freedom go above and beyond. They do absolutely everything to reach their goals, not believing in luck. Sometimes we have to make some hard choices, knowing that the ripple effect is our best friend.

Believe in your version of financial freedom and reach for your goals, and one day you will be able to look back with satisfaction that you did a great job for you and your family.

34 We are all born massively affluent

Opportunity is missed by most people because it is dressed in overalls and looks like hard work

— Thomas Edison

Apart from a few exceptions, most of us can strive to achieve our own version of financial freedom. Yes, some people are born into wealth and obviously have a head-start on the vast majority of us. However, most successful people are self-made.

Here's just a few famous self-made people that have most definitely achieved financial freedom without being given money to start with.

- Richard Branson

- Ralph Lauren

- Steve Jobs

- Bill Gates

These are just a few of them, but there are millions of successful self-made people and you can be one of them too.

One thing they all have in common: They have all had to face adversity and struggled to achieve their successes. They have all had their ups and downs. Success is never a straight line of progression. There are always setbacks that have to be dealt with along the way. The successful do not give up at the first problem; they look at what they are doing, and have had to decide if what they were doing is wrong or not working properly before deciding on their next move. What none of them ever did was decide it was too hard or too difficult. They got on with getting the job done until they got there.

They are often people that have been of great service to others and have not solely focused on their own success. They have strived to serve others.

Someone once said, 'You can have anything you want in this world, so long as you help enough other people get what they want.' Just focusing on the money is not enough and it will only get you so far. The successful are always looking to help others and if you can do this, you too will be successful.

Arnold Schwarzenegger was able to sum up his desire to succeed very simply: 'For me life is continuously being hungry. The meaning of life is not simply to exist, to survive, but to move ahead, to go up, to achieve, to conquer.'

The quote is perhaps somewhat dramatic, but we all need some of that sentiment to make sure that we continue to strive for our goal of financial freedom. It's up to you to find what motivates you to keep reaching for your goals.

On your journey to financial freedom, you will need courage, you will need to be imaginative and sometimes you will need to leave your past opinions behind.

Above all else, I wish you the very best on your onward journey to financial freedom.

Appendix 1

Short-term goals

Medium-term goals

Long-term goals

Appendix 2

How can I reduce my costs?
How can I increase the price?
How can I diversify what I do?
How can I sell more?

Appendix 3

Asset Statement	Asset	Liability
House		
Contents		
Savings		
Investments		
Pensions		
Total		
Net assets		

Appendix 4

Expenditure	
Mortgage	
Council tax	
Gas	
Electricity	
Water	
TV & broadband	
Food	
Eating out	
Birthday gifts	
Christmas gifts	
Gym membership	
Hair	
Holidays	
Pension investment	
Monthly savings	
Monthly total	
Annual total